WHO'S WHO IN FEDERAL POLITICS IN ALBERTA

By

E.G. MARDON, Ph.D.

AUSTIN MARDON

A Golden Meteorite Press Book
© 2011 copyright by Austin Mardon, Edmonton, Canada
All rights reserved. No part of this work may be reproduced in any form or by any means, electronic or mechanical, including photocopying, recording, taping, or any retrieval system, without the written permission of Golden Meteorite Press at aamardon@yahoo.ca.
Printed in Canada by Golden Meteorite Press.
No part of this publication may be reproduced, stored in a retrieval system or transmitted, in any form or by any means, without prior written consent of the publisher or a licence from The Canadian Copyright Licensing Agency (Access Copyright). For an Access Copyright licence, visit www.accesscopyright.ca or call toll free to 1-800-893-5777.

Published by Golden Meteorite Press.
126 Kingsway Garden
Post Office Box 34181,
Edmonton, Alberta, CANADA.
T5G 3G4
Telephone: +1-780-378-0063
Email: aamardon@yahoo.ca

Cover artwork: Lawrence Dommer, 2011

Library and Archives Canada Cataloguing in Publication

Mardon, Ernest G., 1928-
    Who's who in federal politics in Alberta / Ernest G. Mardon.

Includes bibliographical references and index.
ISBN 978-1-897472-19-4

    1. Politicians--Alberta--Biography. 2. Alberta--Politics and government--1905-. 3. Canada--Politics and government--20th century. I. Title.

FC3655.M37 2010   971.23'030922   C2010-905527-6

ISBN 978-1-897472-19-4

Preface

With Canadian regionalism a phenomenon recurring in every period of economic strain since Canadian confederation, questions of the advantages of maintaining a single nation arise. It therefore becomes imperative for us to examine the part which various regions have actually played in the direction of national affairs in Ottawa/ the most disenchanted of these regions of Canada is that of the prairie provinces where recurring protests have been made against eastern economic domination and colonialism. This disenchantment with Ottawa has marked the political and economic development of the region ever since the Prairie Provinces have joined Canada. And one of the most vocal of the three Prairie Provinces has been and remains today the province of Alberta.

This study is primarily a compilation from many sources, chief of which has been the consecutive issues of The Canadian Parliamentary Guide, together with information from newspapers and periodicals in which historical and biographical data has appeared.

There has been no attempt to pass judgment on the total impact and effect that federal politicians from Alberta have had on national policy. But it is the aim of this study to provide the material necessary, for those who are interested, to evaluate the one hundred and fifty individuals who have served Albertans in the national capital and perhaps to use this knowledge in such a way that we will all become more aware of the contribution this province has made on the national scene.

Chapter One

The Lieutenant- Governors

The Lieutenant-Governor is both the representative of the federal government in the Canadian provinces, appointed, instructed and dismissible by it, and the representative of the monarchy insofar as the working of cabinet government is concerned. Since these two aspects are so completely fused in one office, it is often impossible to clearly separate them, and the discretionary powers of the representative of the monarchy may on occasion be used in the interests of the federal government.

Moreover, since the federal government is formed from a political party, it is often difficult to separate the interests of the government from the interests of the party. The province of Alberta and her neighboring prairie province of Saskatchewan were created by an act of the federal government in 1905. (See Appendix One: The Alberta Act)

The first Lieutenant-Governor of Alberta was named by Liberal Prime Minister Wilfrid Laurier. He was George Bulyea, a forty-six year old former cabinet minister in the Haultain administration of the Northwest Territories. He had Liberal affiliations. Bulyea was appointed to a second five-year term in 1910.

The second Lieutenant-Governor was Dr. Robert Brett of Banff. He was named to the position in 1915 by Conservative Prime Minister Robert Borden. He had sat in the Northwest Territories legislature in Regina as the leader for the opposition. He later had served as the president of the Alberta Conservative Association. His successor was another physician, William Egbert. Liberal Prime Minister Mackenzie King named Egbert to the post in 1927. He was an unsuccessful Liberal candidate in the 1910 provincial election.

The fourth person to be appointed to be the king's representative in Alberta was Judge William Walsh. Conservative Prime Minister R.B. Bennett named fellow-Calgarian Walsh to the position in 1931. Walsh had been a Conservative party organizer in 1911, and had allegedly offered David Maloney of St. Albert CPR money if he would run in the constituency.

The only strictly non-political appointment to the post of Lieutenant-Governor in Alberta since 1905 was when Mackenzie King named veteran police officer and Edmonton magistrate Philip Primrose in 1936. Primrose had served thirty years with the Northwest Mounted Police and then twenty years as a magistrate in Edmonton before being named the fifth Lieutenant-Governor. He died in office six months after his appointment.

In 1937 Mackenzie King named a Baptist minister to the vacancy caused by Primrose's death. John Bowen refused to give royal assent to three bills passed by the Alberta legislature in 1937. All the bills were later declared *ultra vires* by the Supreme Court of Canada. John Bowlen, a millionaire Southern Alberta rancher, who was for a time the Liberal leader in the legislature, was named by Prime Minister St. Laurent the Lieutenant-Governor in 1950. He died in 1959 while still in office.

Prime Minster John Diefenbaker appointed J. Percy Page, who had been the acting Progressive Conservative leader in Alberta for several years. Page had been the principal of an Edmonton commercial high school for many years.

The present Lieutenant-Governor is Grant MacEwan who was for years a university professor in Saskatchewan and Manitoba before coming to Alberta in the early 1950s. He was named the provincial Liberal leader after J. Harper Prowse retired in 1959. He also served as mayor of Calgary. Prime Minister Leslie Pearson made this appointment.

The function of the Lieutenant-Governor cannot be abolished. As Lapointe said, he represents law; he represents order; he represents authority. If the Lieutenant-Governor is ill, the provincial Chief Justice of the province takes over his functions, which are mainly honorary, including reading the speech from the throne, giving royal assent to all bills, and proroguing the legislature. To have him act permanently as chief executive officer would serve no useful purpose. The Chief Justice has not the time to perform any ceremonial duties, and the saving to the province would be meager. Whether the executive and judicial branches of the government could be combined presents an interesting legal problem as well.

The Lieutenant-Governors of Alberta in Order of Their Appointment

1905-1915	George H.V. Bulyea, Liberal, Merchant
1915-1927	Robert G. Brett, Conservative, Physician
1927-1931	William Egbert, Liberal, Physician
1931-1936	William L. Walsh, Conservative, Lawyer
1936-1937	Philip H. Primrose, Independent, Soldier
1937-1950	John C. Bowen, Liberal, Minister
1950-1959	John J. Bowlen, Liberal, Rancher
1959-1966	J. Percy Page, Conservative, Educator
1966-	J.W. Grant MacEwan, Liberal, Professor

An Alphabetical List of the Lieutenant-Governors with a Brief Biographical Sketch

John Campbell Bowen, *Minister, 1937-1950*

Born in 1872 at Isgoode Township, Ontario, he was the son of Peter Bowen (Irish). Educated at Brandon College, Manitoba, and McMaster University, he served as a Baptist minister to congregations at Dauphin, Manitoba, Winnipeg and Edmonton prior to 1913. He was for one year secretary of the Board of Education of the Baptist Union of Western Canada. Bowen served as a chaplain with the Canadian Expeditionary Force from 1915 to 1918 in England and France. In 1920, he was elected alderman for the City of Edmonton. The next year he was a successful Liberal candidate for Edmonton in the provincial general election that saw the UFA sweep to power. He failed in a bid for re-election five years later, but was appointed Lieutenant-Governor of Alberta in 1937 when he figured in Social Credit attempted reform measures. Bowen married in 1906, Edith, related to Frank Oliver, M.P. (See: Oliver). They had two daughters. Bowen died in Edmonton in January of 1957.

John J. Bowlen, *Rancher, 1950-1959*

Born in 1876 at Cardigan, Prince Edward Island, he was the son of Michael Bowlen and Mary Casey, both of Irish descent. Educated at public school, he went to Boston as a young man where he was a bus operator before coming to western Canada. He started with sheep, but succeeded with cattle in Southern Alberta. His first entrance into politics was in 1917 when he was the unsuccessful Liberal candidate for federal riding of North Battleford. Bowlen was first elected to the Alberta legislature in 1930 for the multi-member Calgary constituency. He sat in the house for the next fourteen years, being one of the six opposition members to hold his seat in the Aberhart landslide of 1935. He was appointed Lieutenant-Governor in 1950 at the age of seventy four. He was named to a second term, but died in office in 1959. He was a Roman Catholic. He was also a veteran of the Spanish-American War. (See Tony Cashman's *The Vice-Regal Cowboy*, 1958)

Robert George Brett, *Physician, 1915-1927*

He was born in 1851 at Strathroy, Ontario, of pioneer Irish descent. Educated at the University of Toronto, he did post-graduate work in medicine at New York, Philadelphia and Vienna and started practice in Ontario before coming west in 1880. There, he was one of the founders of the Manitoba Medical Centre, and professor at the University of Manitoba. In 1886, Dr. Brett established the Banff Sanatarium, of which he was a medical director. Two years later, he was elected to the Northwest Territories legislature. He served there until 1901, first as president of the executive council and, after autonomy, as leader of the opposition. He was president of the Alberta Conservative Association in 1909. Dr. Brett was

Lieutenant-Governor of Alberta from 1915 to 1927. He died in 1944.

George Hedley Vicars Bulyea, *Merchant, 1905-1915*

Born in 1859 in Gagetown, New Brunswick, he was the son of James Bulyea and Jane Blizzard of United Empire Loyalist stock. He was educated at Gagetown Grammar School and the University of New Brunswick, from which he graduated in 1878 at the head of his class and with honors in Mathematics and French. After teaching for a few years in his native province and serving as principal of Sudbury Grammar School there, he came to western Canada in 1882. Bulyea established himself at Qu'Appelle where he engaged in business as a dealer in furniture and flour and feed until 1898. He was elected a member for Qu'Appelle if the Council of Northwest Territories at Regina in 1894. In 1898, he journeyed to the Yukon as the representative of the Regina legislature. He held a succession of offices in the territorial government, serving as Minister of Agriculture and provincial Secretary, 1898-1903, and as Minister of Public Works, 1903-1905. In 1905, he was appointed first Lieutenant-Governor of Alberta and was re-appointed in 1910. In 1915, he became chairman of the Public Utilities Commission. He died in 1928.

William Egbert, *Physician, 1927-1931*

Born 1857 in Welland County, Upper Canada, he was the son of Joseph Egbert and Maria Silverthorne, born Canadians of United Empire Loyalist descent. Educated at the University of Toronto (M.B. in 1899) and at Victoria University (M.D., C.M.), Egbert taught briefly at Dunville, Ontario, before continuing his medical studies. He came west to Calgary in 1904 to practice medicine. He was an unsuccessful Liberal candidate in the 1910 provincial election, but was elected to the Calgary city council for a two-year term the same year. Egbert was the president of the Alberta Liberal Association from 1917 until 1925 and was appointed Lieutenant-Governor. In 1935, he was chairman of the non-party Economic Safety League, organized to oppose Social Credit. He was a member of The United Church of Canada. He died in 1936 at the age of sixty-seven. His son is a judge of the Alberta Supreme Court.

J.W. Grant MacEwan, *Professor and Author, 1966-Present*

Born in 1902 at Brandon, Manitoba, he was the son of Alex MacEwan and Bertha Grant, both Scottish Canadians. Educated at Brandon, University of Toronto (B.S.A.) and Iowa State College (M.S.), he was a professor at the University of Saskatchewan from 1928 to 1946. He then became Dean of Agriculture, University of Manitoba (1946-1951). He was an unsuccessful Liberal candidate for the federal riding of Brandon in 1951. MacEwan came to Alberta the same year and subsequently was elected a Calgary alderman from 1953 to 1958, and then served as mayor of that city from 1963 to 1965. He served one term in the legislature from 155 to 1959. He succeeded J. Harper Prowse as the Alberta Liberal leader in 1958. He was sworn in an Lieutenant-Governor in 1966. Numerous honors have come to him, among them the honorary degrees conferred by the University of Alberta in 1966, the University of Calgary in 1967, and Brandon University.

MacEwan is the author of twenty books, most of them on various aspects of the history of early western Canada. Among those dealing with Alberta are: *The Sodbusters* (1946), *Between the Red and the Rockies* (1952), *Eye Opener Bob* (1957), *Calgary Cavalcade* (1958), *Fifty Mighty Men* (1958), *John Ware's Cow Country* (1960), *Blazing the Old Cattle Trails* (1962), *Poking into Politics* (1966), and *Harvest of Bread* (1969).

J. Percy Page, *Educator, 1959-1966*

Born 1887 at Rochester, New York, he was the son of Absalom Bell Page, a Canadian. He came to Canada in 1890, where he was educated at Queen's University: B.A. and B.C.S. Page was for many years the principal of the Edmonton Commercial High School and coach of the world champion 'Commercial Grads' basketball team. On the fourth attempt, he was elected to the legislature as a Progressive Conservative for Edmonton in 1952. He was re-elected three years later, but was defeated in the 1959 provincial election. In the same year, Diefenbaker appointed him Lieutenant-Governor to succeed John Bowlen, who had died in office. He retired in 1966. He was a member of The United Church of Canada.

Philip Carteret Hill Primrose, *Soldier, 1936-1937*

Born in Pictou, Nova Scotia, in 1865, he was a distant cousin of the Earl of Roseberry whose family name is Primrose. Educated at the Royal Military College at Kingston, he joined the Northwest Mounted Police as a young man and had a distinguished career with the force in western Canada. He served a total of thirty years with the force, rising to the rank of superintendent. He saw duty in the Yukon at the time of the great gold rush in 1898 and met while there a young lawyer, William Walsh, who later became the fourth Lieutenant-Governor of Alberta. In 1915, he retired from the Mounties to become a magistrate in Edmonton. During the next twenty years, it was said that some 40,000 cases were tried before him. He never participated in politics. Primrose himself considered his appointment to succeed Walsh as the King's representative in Alberta a tribute to the old northwest Mounted Police and its successor, the RCMP. This veteran police office and magistrate was a colorful public figure for half a century in western Canada from the turbulent days of the early 1880s to the depression years of the 1930s. Prime Minister Mackenzie King named him Lieutenant-Governor of Alberta in October, 1936. He died in office some six months later. He was the first northern Albertan to be appointed to the position. His son, Neil D. Primrose, is a judge of the Supreme Court Trial Division of Alberta.

William Legh Walsh, *Lawyer, 1931-1936*

Born in 1857 at Simcoe, Upper Canada, he was the son of Aquila Walsh, who was a member of Parliament for eleven years and who was one of the builders of the Intercolonial Railway. He came of United Empire Loyalist Stock. Educated at the University of Toronto and Osgood Hall, he was called to the Bar in Ontario, 1880. He entered into an association with D'Alton McCarthy in Orangeville, Ontario, the next year. In 1896, Walsh was a successful Conservative candidate for the federal Ontario riding of Cardwell. He served three terms as mayor of Orangeville before coming west in 1900. He established a law practice in Dawson City, Yukon, during the gold rush days. Walsh finally settled in Calgary in 194 and was named a K.C. the same year. He was the first president of the Conservative Association of Alberta and ran unsuccessfully for the party in the first provincial election for the Gleichen constituency. He was a Conservative organizer in the 1911 victory. Appointed a judge of the Supreme Court of Alberta in 1912, Walsh left the bench in 1931 to serve a term as Lieutenant-Governor as of the province. He died in 1938.

Age When Appointed Lieutenant-Governor

Under 50:	1
50 – 59:	nil
60 – 69:	3
70 -79:	5
Average Age:	67

Occupations of Lieutenant-Governors

Merchandising:	1
Agriculture:	1
Medicine:	2
Law:	1
Education:	2
Clergyman:	1
Public Service:	1

Political Experience of Lieutenant-Governors Prior to Appointment

Legislature:	6
Provincial Party leader:	3
Public Service:	1
No Parliamentary experience:	2

The Chief Justices of Alberta

At times when the Lieutenant-Governor cannot fulfill his duties, the Chief Justice of the Appellate Division of the Supreme Court of Alberta takes over. They are therefore included in this work.

List of the Chief Justices of Alberta – 1905 – 1972

Arthur Sifton	1905-1910
Horace Harvey	1910-1921
David L. Scott	1921-1924
Horace Harvey	1924-1949
George B. O'Connor	January 25 1950-1957
Clinton James Ford	January 17 1957-1960
S. Bruce Smith	1960-(Present)

An Alphabetical List of the Chief Justices of Alberta with a Brief Biographical Sketch

Clinton James Ford, *Chief Justice of Alberta 1957-1960*

Born at Corinth, Ontario in 1882, he was educated at the University of Toronto and Osgoode Hall, Toronto, before completing his legal studies in Alberta. He was called to the Alberta Bar in 1910. Ford was named a K.C. in 1921. From 1913 to 1942, he practiced law in Calgary. In the latter year he was appointed a judge of the District Court. In 1945, he was appointed a justice of the Supreme Court of Alberta and five years later transferred to the appellate division. On the death of Chief Justice O'Connor in January 1957, Judge Ford was named Chief Justice of Alberta. He was 75 years of age at the time. He received an honorary doctor of laws degree from the University of Alberta. Ford died in 1961.

Horace Harvey, *Chief Justice of Alberta 1910-1921 and 1924-1949*

Born in Elgin County, Ontario, in 1863, he was the son of William Harvey who was the Liberal Member of Parliament for Elgin East from 1872 until his death two years later, he was educated at the University of Toronto (B.A. 1886; LL.B. 1888). He was called to the Ontario Bar in 1889 before moving west. He was called to the Bar in the Northwest Territories in 1893 and established his law practice in Calgary. Harvey was successfully appointed Registrar of the Land Titles for Southern Alberta in 1869; Deputy Attorney General of the Northwest Territories in 1900; and Puisne Judge of the Territorial Supreme Court in 1904. He was appointed judge of the newly organized Supreme Court of Alberta in 1907. He was invested with the rank of Chief Justice on the retirement of Arthur Sifton in October, 1910, when the former Chief Justice became Alberta's second Premier. Harvey was 47 years old of age at the time.

On reorganization of the courts in 1921, he became Chief Justice of the Trial Division while David Lynch Scott was named Chief Justice. Three years later on the death of Scot, he was appointed Chief Justice of the Appellate Division. Meanwhile, in 1917, he had been named Chairman of the Board of Governors of the University of Alberta. He held this post until 1940.

It was in 1930 that Harvey was assigned one of the most difficult tasks in his career – the problem of investigating the circumstances surrounding the sinking of the schooner Gypsum Queen, sunk off the west coast of Ireland allegedly after being torpedoed by a German U-boat during the Great War. He died at the advanced age of 86. He was the last of the officials carried over into Alberta from the Territorial days. Chief Justice Harvey was scholarly, studious and dignified. He had an analytical mind and always got down to the roots in hearing cases in the Trial Court or reviewing judgments in the Appellate Court. He was an Anglican.

George Bligh O'Connor, Chief Justice of Alberta, 1950-1957

Born at Walkerton, Ontario, in 1883, he was educated at Walkerton and Osgoode Hall, Toronto (silver medal 1905). O'Connor was called to the Ontario and Alberta Bars in 1905 when he joined W.A. Griesbach in forming a law firm in Edmonton. He was named a K.C. in 1913 and became one of the prominent lawyers in Alberta's capital. He was appointed a justice of the Supreme Court of Alberta in 1941, and five years later was appointed to Appeal Court. He served on several important inquiries. Including the 1941 Royal Commission into wages paid to coal miners. He was also Chairman of the Wartime Labor Relations board. In 1950, on the death of Horace Harvey, O'Connor was named Chief Justice of

Alberta. He was 67 years of age at the time. He died in January 1957; he was an Anglican.

David Lynch Scott, Chief Justice of Alberta 1921-1924

Born at Brampton, Upper Canada in 1845, he was educated at the Brampton grammar school, and called to the Ontario Bar in 1870. He practiced law, first in Orangeville, Ontario, and after 1882 in Regina, Northwest Territories. He was the first mayor of Regina in 1883 and organized a volunteer corps for home duty during the Indian and Metis revolt two years later. Scott was one of the Counsel for the Crown at the trial of Louis Riel. The Crown demanded the death penalty for the high treason for Riel, though it has been said that the shooting of Orangeman Thomas Scott in March 1870, during the Red River Rebellion was the real reason why the Ontario Orangemen wanted Riel slain. Riel was hanged at the N.W.M.P. barracks in November 1885. The portrait of the Corwn Prosecutor, David Lynch Scott, hangs in the Court House at Regina today. For his services in connection with this trial, Scott was named a Q.C., and nine years later, he was raised to the bench in the Northwest territories. In 1905, he was transferred to the bench of Alberta, and on the reorganization of the courts in 1921, was appointed Chief Justice of the province. He was seventy-six years of age at the time. He died at South Cooking Lake, Alberta in July 1924. He was an Anglican.

Arthur Sifton, *Chief Justice of Alberta, 1906-1910*

(See list of Members of Parliament)

Sidney Bruce Smith, *Chief Justice of Alberta 1961-Present*

Born at Toronto at 1899, he was the son of Frederick Howard Smith and Kate Smith (nee Marks). He was educated at the University of Alberta (B.A. 1919; LL.B. 1922 – gold medalist). Bruce Smith read law with Frank Ford of Edmonton before being called to the Bar of Alberta in 1922. He practiced law in Alberta for many years. He served on the Edmonton Public School Board from 1947 to 1941. Prime Minister Diefenbaker in 1958 named him Chairman of the Board of Transport Commissioners for Canada. A year later, he was appointed judge of the Trial Division of the Supreme Court of Alberta. On the death of Chief Justice Ford, Bruce Smith was appointed Chief Justice of Alberta in February 1961. He was sixty-one years of age at the time. In 1962 he was awarded an honorary degree from the University of Alberta. He was an Anglican.

Chapter Two

The Senators: The Senate

While the Senate possesses legal power almost equal to that of the House of Commons, and in theory an independent legislative body, it is in actual practice a minor partner in the legislature. Three constitutional principles emphasize this fact, the first two explicit, and the third unwritten. These three principles are that: only the House of Commons is based on popular election; the House of Commons has the sole power to originate money bills; and the cabinet is responsible to the House of Commons and not to the Senate.

The main functions and duties of the Senate are to act as a revising and restraining body and to protect the interest of the provinces and minority racial, religious and language groups.

The first great handicap which was placed on the Senate at Confederation was the system under which its members were appointed.. with only a few notable exceptions, appointments to the Red Chamber have been made by the Prime Minister of the day to faithful party supporters. Goldwin Smith states, "The Senate is a bribery fund in the hands of the government, and paddock for the 'Old War Horse' of the party, nor, on its present footing will it ever be anything else; ... A minister cannot help himself; the goods in the shape of party services and expenditures on elections have been delivered, and he is compelled to pay."

Under the Alberta Act of 1905, Alberta was to have four Senators. This number was increased to six in 1915. There have been a total of twenty-five Albertans summoned to the Senate since 1905. Of these, seventeen have been Liberals, four Conservatives, one Social Credit (Manning), one Independent Conservative (Gladstone), one Independent Liberal (Cameron), and one Independent (Burns).

Senators from the Province of Alberta In Order of Appointment

According to the Alberta Act which created the province in 1905, the newly-created province had the right to have four Senators.

James Lougheed, of Calgary, Conservative (1888-1925)

Philippe Roy, of Edmonton, Liberal (1906-1911)

Peter Talbot, of Lacombe, former Liberal MP for Alberta (1906-1919)

Dr. L. George De Veber, of Lethbridge, former Liberal MLA (1906-1925)

Amedee Forget, of Banff, Liberal (1911-1923)

The number of Senators from Alberta was increased to six in 1915.

Edward Michener, of Red Deer, former Conservative MLA (1918-1948)

W.J. Harner, of Edmonton (1918-1948)

W.A. Griesbach, of Edmonton, former Conservative MP (1921-1944)

J.L. Cote, of Edmonton, former Liberal MLA (1923-1924)

William A. Buchanan, of Lethbridge, former Liberal MLA and MP (1925-1954)

P.E. Lessard, of St. Paul, former Liberal MLA (1924-1931)

Daniel E. Riley, of High River, Liberal (1926-1943)

Pat Burns, of Calgary, Independent (1931-1936)

Dr. Aristide Blais, of Edmonton, Liberal (1940-1963)

Dr. Frederick Gershaw, of Medicine Hat, former Liberal MP (1945-1963)

G.H. Ross, of Calgary, former Liberal MP (1948-1958)

James A. MacKinnon, of Edmonton, former Liberal MP (1949-1958)

J. Wesley Stambaugh, of Bruce, Liberal (1949-1963)

Donald Cameron, of Banff, Independent Liberal (1955-   )

James Gladstone, of Lethbridge, Independent Conservative (1958-1971)

John A. Buchanan, of Edmonton, Progressive Conservative (1958-1971)

Harry Hays, former Liberal MP (1966-   )

Earl Hastings, of Calgary, Liberal (1966-   )

J. Harper Prowse, former Liberal MLA (1966-   )

Ernest C. Manning, of Edmonton, Social Credit (1970-   )

The extent to which the representatives from Alberta in the Senate have been recruited from the House of Commons and the legislature can best be illustrated by the following table:

Political Experience of Senators Before Appointment

House of Commons	7
Legislature	8
Federal Minister	3
Provincial Minister	5
Provincial Party Leader	2
Premier	1
No Parliamentary experience	11

Age When Appointed to the Senate

30-39	2
40-49	5
50-59	6
60-69	6
70-	6

Occupations of Alberta Senators

Finance, Insurance, Business	3
Agriculture	6
Engineering, Construction, Mining	3

Medicine	4
Law	4
Education	1
Press, Publication	1
Public Service	3

Senators From Alberta

1905 – 1972

Biographical sketches of each of the twenty-six citizens of the province have who been named to the Upper Chamber of the Canadian Parliament.

Dr. Aristide Blais, *of Edmonton, Liberal, Surgeon (Summoned to the Senate in 1940)*

He was born in 1875 at Berthier, Quebec, the son of Narcisse Blais and Philomene Buteau, both French-Canadians. Educated at Laval University (B.Sc., M.D.) he served as a medical officer in France during the Great War. He was surgeon and chief surgeon at the General Hospital in Edmonton for many years. Dr. Blais was a Roman Catholic, and he died in 1964.

John Alexander (Buck) Buchanan, *of Edmonton, Progressive Conservative, Engineer (Summoned to the Senate in January 1959)*

He was born at Comber, Ontario, in 1887 and educated there. At the University of Toronto he obtained a civil engineering degree in 1909 and worked for years in the Northwest Territories as an engineer. Later, he moved to Edmonton where he became president of Buchanan Construction and Engineering Company. He was an unsuccessful

Conservative candidate in the 1930 provincial election. Buchanan resigned from the Senate in October 1965. He was Protestant.

William Ashbury Buchanan – *MLA for Lethbridge, (1909-1910); Minister without Portfolio, (1909-1911); M.P. for Medicine Hat, (1911-1917); M.P. for Lethbridge, (1917-1921); Senator from Alberta, (1925-1954)*

Born at Fraserville, Ontario, in 1876, he was the son of Rev. William Buchanan and Mary Pendrie, and he commenced his long newspaper career by working as a reporter on several Ontario newspapers. In 1905, he came west and bought a half-interest in *The Lethbridge Herald*, a weekly. He converted it into a daily and soon became the sole owner. In 1907, he organized the first legislative library in Edmonton. He was elected to the provincial house in 1909, and was taken into the Rutherford cabinet. (He was the only cabinet minister that has ever been named from Lethbridge). Two years later, he entered federal politics when he defeated the sitting member for Medicine Hat, Charles Magrath, the first mayor of Lethbridge. He was re-elected in 1917 for the newly-created Lethbridge riding. In 1925, he was named to the Senate. Under his guidance, *The Lethbridge Herald* acquired a widespread reputation for public and regional service, encouraging the building of railways, irrigation works, highways and public parks. Religion: Methodist. Buchanan was one of the most influential Liberals in Western Canada for many years. He died in Lethbridge in 1954.

Patrick Burns, *of Calgary, Independent Conservative, Rancher (Senator from Alberta 1931-1936)*

Born at Oshawa, Ontario, in 1856, of Irish descent, he came west to Manitoba as a young man and went into business for himself as a cattle dealer. In 1890, he arrived in Calgary where he acquired his ranch and established a meat packing firm. In the course of time it became one of the largest businesses of its kind in the world. In 1912 Burns, who was better known as Pat or merely P.B., was one of the financial backers for the first Calgary stampede. He held directorships in a number of banking, insurance and engineering firms. He was Calgary's first industrial millionaire tycoon. Prime Minister R.B. Bennett, who had known Burns for thirty-five years, made the first non-political appointment to the Senate when he summoned the Calgarian to the Upper Chamber. He resigned his seat in 1936 and died a few months later at the age of eighty years.

Donald Cameron, *of Banff, Independent Liberal, Educator (Summoned to the Senate in 1955)*

Born in 1903 at Devonport, England, his family came to Canada in 1906. He was the son of Donald

Cameron, who was the UFA member of the legislature for Innisfail from 1921 to 1935. He was educated at Lakeview and the University of Alberta (B.Sc. 1930; M.Sc. 1934). He received an LL.D. degree (Honoris Causa) from the University of British Columbia in 1959. He married Stella Mary Ewing of Calgary. Cameron was the Director of Extension, University of Alberta, for twenty years, 1936-1956, and Director of the Banff School of Fine Arts from 1936 to the present. He was the chairman of a Royal Commission on Education in Alberta in the late 1950s. He is the author of *Campus in the Clouds*. He is a member of The United Church of Canada.

Jean Leon Cote, *of Edmonton, Liberal, Civil Engineer and Surveyor; MLA for Athabasca, (1909-1913); MLA for Grouard, (1913-1924); Provincial Secretary (1918-1921), Senator from Alberta (1923-1924)*

Born at Les Eboulements, Quebec, in 1867, he was of French Canadian descent. He was educated at the commercial academy at Montmagny, Quebec. He worked as a land surveyor for the federal Department of the Interior from 1893 to 1900. He then became the director of several companies, including Jasper Colleries, and his own mining and engineering firm. He entered provincial politics when he ran as a Liberal candidate for Athabasca in 1909. He was elected and re-elected for constituency of Grouard in the general elections of 1913, 1917, and 1921. He served in Premier Charles Stewart's cabinet as the Provincial Secretary from 1918 until it was defeated by the United Farmers of Alberta three years later. He was appointed to the Senate by Mackenzie King in August 1923, but died a year later. He was a Roman Catholic.

Dr. Leverett George De Veber, *of Lethbridge, Liberal, Physician; MLA for the Northwest Territories (1898-1905); MLA for Lethbridge (1905-1906); Minister without portfolio (1905-1906); Senator from Alberta (1906-1919)*

Born at St. John, New Brunswick, in 1848, he was of United Empire Loyalist stock. He was educated at King's College, Windsor, Nova Scotia, and Bartholomew Hospital, London, from where he graduated in 1870. He came to western Canada with the Northwest Mounted Police to which force he was named staff surgeon. He started a private practice in Macleod but moved to Lethbridge 1890. Dr. De Veber is among the first physicians to come to Alberta. For a number of years he was the health officer for the city of Lethbridge. He entered territorial politics as a Liberal when he was elected by acclamation to represent the area in the Regina legislature. He was named to the first Alberta cabinet formed by Rutherford as a Minister without Portfolio. However, within a year he was appointed to the Senate by Wilfrid Laurier. He died in July 1925.

Amedee Emmanuel Forget, *of Banff, Liberal, Lawyer (Summoned to the Senate in 1911)*

He was born in 1847 at Mariaville, Quebec. Called to the Bar in 1871, he served for some years as secretary of the Council of the Bar for Montreal. He then entered the Dominion civil service and was one of the commissioners for the settlement of the Metis claims in 1885 in the Northwest Territories in 1898. He still held this position when the provinces of Alberta and Saskatchewan were created by the act of the federal parliament. He was then appointed the first Lieutenant-Governor if Saskatchewan (1905-1910). Moving to Alberta, he settled at Banff whence he was named to the Upper Chamber. Forget died in June 1923 at Ottawa.

Dr. Frederick W. Gershaw, *of Medicine Hat, Liberal, Physician; MP for Medicine Hat 1925-1935 and 1940-1945; Senator from Alberta 1945-1963*

Born at Emerson, Manitoba in 1883, he was of German descent. He was educated at Emerson and the University of Manitoba where he obtained a medical degree. He established his practice in Medicine Hat and was a popular physician for many years. He was keen on southern Alberta history, and was the author of several works. Dr. Gershaw entered federal politics in 1921 when he ran as a Liberal and failed to get elected. He was, however, successful four years later. He represented Medicine Hat in the Commons for fifteen years before he was appointed to the Senate by Mackenzie King in 1945. Religion: United Church.

James Gladstone, *of Lethbridge, Independent Conservative, Farmer; Summoned to the Senate by Diefenbaker in 1958-1971*

He had the distinction of being the first Tory Indian to be appointed to the Upper Chamber. Born in 1887 near Mountain Mill, Alberta, he was the son of William Gladstone, a trader, and Harriet LeBlanc, Blood Indian, and was raised and educated at St. Paul's Anglican Mission on the Blood Reserve. Married in 1911 to Janie, daughter of Potaina of the Blood tribe, Gladstone was active for many years in the Indian Association of Alberta. He died in 1971. He was an Anglican.

William Antrobus Griesbach, *of Edmonton, Conservative, Soldier; Senator from Alberta 1921-1945*

Born at Fort Qu'Appelle, Saskatchewan, in 1878, he was the son of Colonel Arthur Griesbach of the Northwest Mounted Police. He was educated at St. John's College, Winnipeg. He served in the Canadian Mounted RIfels in the South African War with General Stewart of Lethbridge and Colonel Jamieson of Edmonton – all three were active Conservatives. On his return, he was called to the Alberta Bar in 1901. Griesbach first entered civic politics. He was elected alderman in 1905 and 1913. He also tried to get elected to the House of Commons in 1911 but was defeated. Non the outbreak of the Great War he volunteered for service in the Canadian Expeditionary Force and saw active duty in France. He received rapid promotion and was awarded the DSO and bar, CMG and CB besides being mentioned in dispatches six times. In the federal election of 1917, he was finally successful in being elected to the Commons as the member for Edmonton West. In so doing, he defeated Liberal Frank Oliver, who had served six years in Laurier's cabinet. Griesbach was trailing by eighty votes after the civilian votes had been tallied/ the military votes gave him close to a 3,000-vote majority when they had been included. He was named a King's Council in 1919 and appointed to the Senate by Prime Minister Arthur Meighan in 1921. Griesbach was named Inspector General for western Canada in 1940. He died in January 1945 in Edmonton. He was an Anglican. His autobiography, *I Remember*, was published by Ryerson Press in 1946.

Richard Hardisty, *of Edmonton, Conservative, Chief Factor; Senator from the Northwest Territories 1888-1889*

Born in 1831, he was educated at St. John's College, Winnipeg. Hardisty, like his grandfather and father before him, was for many years Chief Factor of the Hudson's Bay Company in charge of the Edmonton district. He was an unsuccessful Conservative candidate for the federal house from the Northwest Territories rising of Alberta in 1887. Sir John A. MacDonald named him to the Red Chamber a year later. However, Senator Hardisty drowned in 1889, following an accident while traveling from Prince Albert to Qu'Appelle by wagon. His niece's husband, thirty-five year old James Lougheed, was named to the Senate as his replacement.

William J. Harmer, *of Edmonton, Liberal, Civil Servant; Senator from Alberta from 1918-1947*

Born at Fort Frontenace (Kingston), Ontario, in 1872, he was the son of James Harmer who was of English descent. Educated at Napanee, he came west in 1891 to join the railway operating traffic department. He rose rapidly in the provincial civil service and was the Deputy Minister of Railways from 1905 until he was named to the Senate thirteen years later. The Calgary Herald called his appointment an "unpleasant surprise... Mr. Harmer has performed no public action, nor has he attained any public or personal distinction... His record is that of a civil servant of very ordinary ability, whose chief and almost only function has been to act as a political manager for Hon. A.L. Sifton." It is said that the Senator did not speak even once in the twenty-nine years he sat in the Red Chamber. He died in September 1947 at Napanee, Ontario.

Earl Adam Hastings, *of Pallister-Foothills, Liberal, Petroleum Landman; Senator from Alberta 1966-Present*

Born at Regina in 1924, he was educated at Wetmore and Regina College. He joined the Canadian Air Force in 1942 and saw active service in Europe. He attained the rank of pilot officer. On his return to Canada, he became the executive assistant to the leader of the Saskatchewan Liberal party, a position he held for six years. In 1952, he joined the Sun Oil Company and became a petroleum landman. Hastings was always interested in politics. He ran against Eldon Woolliams, PC, a member of parliament for Bow River in the 1962 and 1963 general elections, but was defeated both times. Religion: United Church.

Harry William Hays, *of Calgary, Liberal, Rancher; Senator from Alberta 1966-Present; Minster of Agriculture 1963-1965*

Born at Carstairs, Alberta, in 1909, he was the son of Dr. Thomas Hays and Ambriss Foster. He was educated at Glenmore and Calgary. He is a wealthy rancher. Hays was the mayor of Calgary from 1959 to 1963 when he entered federal politics. He won the Calgary South riding and was named by Prime Minister Lester Pearson to the cabinet Minister of Agriculture. He only sat in parliament two years before being defeated in the 1965 election. In 1966, Pearson appointed him to the Upper Chamber. He is a Roman Catholic.

Prosper-Edmond Lessard, *of St. Paul, Liberal, Merchant; MLA for Pakan and then St. Paul 1909-1921; Provincial Minister without Portfolio 1909-1910; Senator from Alberta 1925-1931*

Born at Cranbourne, Quebec, in 1873, he was the son of Jean Lessard and Annie Davidson, both Canadians. He was educated at Ste. Anne de la

Pocatiere and Mount St. Louis Colleges. He came west to Edmonton as a young man in 1898. He married Helen, daughter of Joseph H. Gariepy of Edmonton. He became a wholesale merchant. Lessard was an Edmonton separate school trustee for several years. He then entered provincial politics as a Liberal for the Pakan constituency. He was in Rutherford's cabinet as a Minister without Portfolio for a year. He sat in the Legislature from 1909 to 1921. After he was defeated, he was still active in politics. He was the Liberal party Edmonton president when he was named to the Senate by Mackenzie King in 1925 to fill the position that had become vacant on the death of Senator Jean Cote. He died in April 1930 at St. Paul. He was a Roman Catholic.

Sir James Lougheed, *of Calgary, Conservative, Lawyer; Senator from Alberta 1889-1925*

Born in Brampton, Ontario in 1854, he was the son of a building contractor and as a young man worked as a carpenter before obtaining a law degree from Osgoode Hall. He was called to the Ontario Bar in 1881 and practiced briefly in Toronto before moving west. He arrived in Calgary two years later on foot and was the first lawyer to establish himself on the banks of the Bow River. In 1884, Lougheed married Belle Hardisty, daughter of William Hardisty and niece of both Senator Richard Hardisty and Lord Strathcona. When Senator Hardisty died following an accident five years later, the thirty five year old Calgary lawyer was appointed to succeed him in the

Senate. When Lougheed took his eat, he was the youngest member of the Upper Chamber. In 1906, he became the opposition leader in the Senate and five years later, he was brought into Borden's Conservative cabinet as Minister without Portfolio. Later, in Prime Minister Arthur Meighen's cabinet of 1920, Senator Lougheed was the Minister of the Interior. It was said many times in his later years, that he would have been Prime Minister had he been in the Commons. He was Anglican. Premier Peter Lougheed is his grandson.

James Angus MacKinnon, *of Edmonton, Liberal, Investment Dealer; Senator from Alberta 1949-1957*

Born at Port Elgin, Ontario, in 1881, he was the son of James MacKinnon and Margaret Tolmie, both of British descent. He was educated locally and taught briefly in Ontario and Alberta before he settled in Edmonton where he became a reporter for *The Edmonton Bulletin*. In 1911, he went into the insurance business as managing director of James A. MacKinnon of which he was the president for many years. He also held directorships in several other important corporations. Entering federal politics in 1935, he ran in the Edmonton West riding, which had been held by Charles Stewart for a number of years. He was elected and remained in the Commons until he was appointed to the Senate fourteen years later. From 1935 to 1939, Alberta did not have a representative on the federal cabinet. In the later year, MacKinnon was brought into Mackenzie King's cabinet as a Minister without Portfolio, and held successive appointments as Minister of Trade and Commerce, 1940-1948; Minister of Fisheries, 1948; and Minister of Mines and Resources, 1948-1949. From April, 1949, until his resignation from the cabinet in December, 1950, he was once again Minister without Portfolio. Religion: Presbyterian.

Ernest Charles Manning, *of Edmonton, Social Credit, Minister; MLA for Calgary and then Edmonton 1935-1968; Provincial Secretary 1935-1943; Minister of Trade and Industry 1935-1943; Premier of Alberta 1943-1968; Provincial Treasurer 1944-1954; Minister of Mines and Minerals 1952-1962; Attorney General 1955-1966; Senator from Alberta 1970-Present*

Born at Carnduff, Saskatchewan in 1908, he was the son of George manning and Elizabeth Dickson, both Britishers. He was educated at Rosetown, Saskatchewan and the Prophetic Bible Institute in Calgary. As a young man, he came under the influence of William "Bible Bill" Aberhart and was closely associated with him as teacher of fundamentalist Christianity and later as advocate of the Social Credit candidate and after being elected was taken into Aberhart's cabinet. In the Premier's death eight years later, Manning was chosen by the Social Credit members of the legislature to be Aberhart's successor. He was the dominant figure in Alberta politics for thirty five years/he retired from provincial politics in December 1969 after serving to the Senate in October 1970. He received an honorary degree from the University of Lethbridge in 1972.

Edward Michener, *of Red Deer, Conservative, Financial Broker; MLA for Red Deer 1909-1918; Alberta leader of the Conservative Party 1911-1918; Senator from Alberta 1918-1945*

Born at Tintern, Lincoln County, Ontario in 1869, he was the son of Jacob Michener and Eliza Michener. He was educated at St. Catherine's Collegiate Institute, Victoria University, Toronto, and at Wesley College, Winnipeg. He married in 1897 Mary Roland. They had four sons and four daughters. (One of his sons, Roland Michener, was sworn in as the Governor General of Canada on April 17, 1967). Michener was a financial broker and became active in civic politics in Red Deer where he settled. He was mayor of the town on three different occasions. He entered provincial politics in 1909 when he ran as the Conservative candidate in Red Deer. He represented the constituency in the legislature for the next ten years. After R.B. Bennett entered federal politics in 1911, he became the leader of the Alberta Conservative party. Robert Borden appointed him to the Senate in 1918. Religion: Methodist. He died in June 1947, at the age of seventy eight years.

J. Harper Prowse, *of Edmonton, Liberal, Lawyer; Senator from Alberta 1966-Present*

Born at Taber, Alberta in 1913, he was the son of J.H. Prowse who was of British descent. He was educated at Taber and the University of Alberta, where he obtained a B.A. and an LL.B. degree. He worked as a teacher (1931-1934) and as a newspaper reporter when he was a young man before joining the Canadian Army. He saw active service with the Loyal Edmonton Regiment in Italy during the Second World War, and attained the rank of captain. He was elected tot eh legislature in 1945 to represent Albertans who were serving in the Canadian Army. He sat as an Independent during his first term. He joined the Liberal party in 1948 and became the Liberal provincial leader, a position he held for the next ten years. He failed in his attempt to defeat Premier Manning's Social Credit administration, although he led a large opposition party following the 1955 election. He was unsuccessful in his efforts to be elected to the Commons. In 1985, he resigned as party leader to devote more time to his law practice. He ran against incumbent Marcel Lambert in Edmonton West in 1962 and 1963. He was appointed by Prime Minister Pearson in 1966 to the Senate.

Daniel Edward Riley, *of High River, Liberal Rancher; Senator from Alberta 1926-1948*

Born at Baltic, Prince Edward Island in 1860, he was educated at normal school, Charlottetown. He moved to Alberta in 1882, and was a pioneer rancher in the High River district. He also founded the real estate and insurance firm of D.E. Riley and Sons in 1900. Six years later, he was elected the first mayor of High River. Riley was an unsuccessful Liberal candidate in the 1917 general election. He was called to the Senate in 1926. He died in April of 1948, at Calgary. Religion: Presbyterian.

George Henry Ross, *of Calgary, Liberal, Lawyer; Senator from Alberta 1948-1958*

Born at Bedeque, Prince Edward Island in 1878, and educated at Michigan University where he obtained an LL.B. In 1911, he married May, the daughter of David McDougall of Morley, Alberta. As a young man, he settled in Calgary where he practiced law for many years. He was an unsuccessful Liberal candidate in the provincial election of 1913, but was created K.C. In 1940, he was the Liberal candidate for the federal riding of Calgary East and defeated the incumbent Social Crediter, John Landeryou, by 485 votes. He was named to the Upper Chamber in 1948. Ross died in September, 1956, at Calgary.

Dr. Philippe Roy, *of Edmonton, Liberal, Physician; Senator from Alberta 1906-1911*

Born at St. Francois, Quebec in 1868, he was the son of G.B. Roy and Josephine Vallieres, both French Canadians. He was educated at the College Ste. Anne de la Pocatiere and Laval University where he obtained a medical degree in 1889. He came west and settled in Edmonton where he developed a successful practice. He also became the managing director of Le Courrier de l'Ouest, a French language newspaper. Dr. Roy was largely interested in extending the work and influence of French immigration and French capital to Canada. He was anti-clerical and a strong supporter of Wilfrid Laurier, who was Prime Minister from 1896 to 1911. He was appointed to the Senate in 1906 as one of Alberta's new Senators. Dr. Roy resigned his seat in the Upper Chamber in 1911 upon his appointment as Commissaire General du Canada en France and took up residence in Paris. He replaced another former Senator, Hector Fabre, who had held the post for thirty years/ the status of the post was raised to that of Envoy Extraordinary and Minister Plenipotentiary to France in 1928. Roy retired in December 1938, and died ten years later at Ottawa.

J. Welsey Stambaugh, *of Bruce, Liberal, Farmer; Senator from Alberta 1949-1964*

Born at Melvin, Michigan in 1888, he was the son of Rev. Albert Stambaugh, a Methodist minister, and Christine Zimmerman. After receiving his education in the United States he came to Canada in 1905, and homesteaded in the Bruce district. In 1912, he married Amy Lake of Moscow, Ontario. He was the president of the Liberal Association of Alberta when he was called to the Senate in 1949. He retired from the Senate in 1964. Religion: United Church.

Peter Talbot, *of Strathcona, Liberal, Farmer; Senator from Alberta 1905-1918*

Born at Eramosa, Ontario in 1854, he was of Scottish descent. Educated at Ottawa normal school, he obtained a first class teaching certificate and taught at Cornwall in the 1880s before coming west, he was principal of Macleod Public School 1890-1892, and Justice of the Peace there for ten years. Talbot was elected ti the Regina parliament in 1902 as a supporter of the Haultain government. Two years later, he won the newly-created Strathcona riding for the Liberals. Talbot could have become the first Premier of Alberta but declined the honor. He was the not a wealthy man and professed to find the hurly-burly of politics beyond his means and strength. In 1906, he was named to the Upper Chamber by Laurier as one of the new Senators from Alberta. He was fifty-two years of age at this time. Talbot died December 6, 1919, at Lacombe.

Senators from Alberta since 1905

Date					
1889			Lougheed (Cons)		
1906	Talbot (Lib)	Roy (Lib)		De Veber (Lib)	
1911		Forget (Lib)			
1918	Harmer (Lib)				Michener (Cons)
1921		Griesbach (Cons)			
1923	Cote (Lib)				
1925	Lessard (Lib)		Buchanan (WA) (Lib)	Riley (Lib)	
1931	Burns (Indep)				
1940	Blais (Lib)				
1945		Gershaw (Lib)			

Year							
1949	MacKinnon (Lib)					Ross (Lib)	Stambaugh (Lib)
1955				Cameron (Ind. Lib.)			
1958	J. Buchanan (PC)					Gladstone (Ind. Cons)	
1966	Prowse (Lib)	Hays (Lib)	Hastings (Lib)				
1970							Manning (SC)

Chapter Three

Elective Representatives from Alberta

The House of Commons

The House of Commons is the real centre of parliamentary authority and exercises a preponderant influence in the government. It is the organized medium through which the public finds expression and exercises its ultimate political power. It forms the indispensable part of the legislature and it is the body to which the executive must turn for justification and approval. It is based on popular election and, basically, representation by population determines the number of seats allotted to each province, with provision for adjustment after each decennial census.

There has been a total of one hundred and twenty members of Parliament elected since 1905 to represent the province in Ottawa: forty-six Conservatives, thirty-four Liberals, twenty-eight Social Crediters (two of them crossing party lines – one to join the Conservatives [Robert Thompson of Red Deer] and the other the Liberals [Bud Olson of Medicine Hat]), and fourteen United Farmers of Alberta. Douglas Harkness, P.C., has represented Calgary in Ottawa for a longer period of time than any other M.P. – a total of twenty-seven years.

The number of ridings in the province has increased from four in 1904 to nineteen as of the last federal election in 1963. (See Maps showing the changes in the boundaries of the Ridings).

The Early years 1905-1921

When Alberta was created by act of Parliament, it was sending four members to Ottawa: two Conservatives and two Liberals. In 1908, the province's representation was increased to seven: three were Conservatives and four were Liberals. In the 1911 general election that saw Robert Borden and the Conservatives takes power for the first time in fifteen years, Alberta did not go with the rest of Canada. It sent six Liberals to Ottawa, and the only Conservative was R.B. Bennett, the Calgary lawyer who was to become the Prime Minister of Canada some twenty years later.

In the war-time election of 1917, Alberta sent a total of eleven supporters of Borden's national government to Ottawa. Only one Laurier Liberal was elected.

The Reign of the United Farmers of Alberta 1921-1935

In the 1921 federal election, the United Farmers of Alberta and their allies were successful in capturing all the ridings. It was the first time that Alberta turned her back on the old line parties. It was not until thirty-seven years later when John Diefenbaker, a prairie lawyer, was the leader of the Progressive Conservative party, that voters again cast their ballots in a significant number for either Conservatives or

Liberals. In the federal elections in 1925, 1926 and 1930, the rural areas of the province remained faithful to Henry Wise Wood's agrarian protest movement.

The Social Credit Era 1935-1958

The Social Credit movement was never much of a political success in Britain, the country in which the doctrine was formulated in the early 1920s by a mechanical engineer, Major C.H. Douglas. But it took firm root on the Canadian prairies, especially in Alberta after William "Bible Bill" Aberhart, a Calgary school principal and fundamental lay preacher became an ardent supporter. The Douglas doctrine was first propagated in the province through the United Farmers of Alberta. Yet despite many efforts, the U.F.A. finally refused to make it part of their platform.

Douglas' ideas were examined in a large number of study groups across the province. And Aberhart discussed Social Credit theory through his Calgary Prophetic Bible Institute and his weekly Sunday radio broadcasts, which had begun in 1926. Like their leader, his religious following quickly found in social credit a solution to the great economic problems of the depression.

Though at first Aberhart was opposed to political action, the many social credit study groups that were mushrooming throughout Alberta. They soon became restive, and the developing movement rapidly engaged in action; so fast, in fact, that in the provincial election of 1935, the movement found itself with candidates in all constituencies of the province. By election night, still without a party leader because Aberhart had refused to run, the group had been mandated by fifty-four percent of the voters and held 56 of the 63 seats in the legislature.

Social Credit, a few weeks later, became a political force in federal politics. The movement sent seventeen deputies to Ottawa in the 1935 general election – fifteen of them from Alberta. They sat as a western protest group in the federal Parliament for the next twenty-three years.

During this period, a total of forty-nine members of Parliament were sent to Ottawa. Of them, twenty-nine belonged to the Social Credit group. The Liberals who were the party in power in Ottawa until June 1957 elected eleven members and the Conservatives only nine. The only real opposition to the Social Credit party during all this time came from the two cities of Edmonton and Calgary. John Blackmore of Lethbridge led the Social Credit group in Ottawa for the first ten years, and the Solon Low, a former Provincial Treasurer and Minister of Education in the provincial administrations of Aberhart, and after his death, Ernest Manning, became the Social Credit national leader. The Social Credit party was wiped out federally in the Diefenbaker landslide of 1958.

In the federal election held the same year, Social Crediters captured fifteen of Alberta's seventeen ridings. During the next twenty-three years, the party's representation in Ottawa never fell below ten. The voters, especially in the rural areas, supported SoCred candidates until the March 1958 election that saw John Diefenbaker's Progressive Conservatives sweep the province.

The Diefenbaker Years 1958-Present

In the four federal elections held during the 1960s, the Progressive Conservatives held the vast majority of the seats. The votes remained faithful to Diefenbaker when they turned to the Liberals in other parts of the country. Even when Robert Stanfield took over as the leader of the Tory party, the majority of seats remained Conservative. In the 1968 election, when the Social Credit as a federal force in Alberta was in eclipse after their leader, Robert Thompson, joined the Conservatives and Bud Olson, their only federal member joined the Liberals, the Progressive Conservatives elected their candidates in fifteen of the nineteen ridings. Trudeau mania that raged in other parts of the nation did not seem to affect Albertans in large numbers.

Occupations of Alberta's Members of Parliament

Farming	35
Law	26
Business	20
Education	14
Medicine	10
Publishing	6
Public Service	5
Clerical	5

Merchandising	4
Ministry	2
Accounting	2
Engineering	1
Military Service	20
Women	1

Members of the House of Commons, (M.P.)

Elected from Alberta Constituencies

From 1905 to 1972

Herbert Bealey Adshead, *Independent labor for Calgary East 1926-1930*

Born near Manchester, England in 1862, he was educated art Manchester Grammar School. He came to Canada in 1878 and four years later, married Ellen S. Unwin of Madoc, Ontario, a relative of the Unwin Brothers, Publishers of London, England. He obtained a teaching certificate from the Ottawa normal school and taught for several years near Olds, Alberta, while homesteading at the same time. Finally, rented his farm in 1912 and moved to Calgary, where he entered civic politics. He was elected to the city council four times, and in 1917, he was defeated in his attempt to become the mayor by only ten votes, e stood for the Legislature as an Independent farmer in 1921, but was defeated. His political affiliation changed from Liberal to right-wing Labor. He was elected for Calgary East in the federal election of 1926 as a Labor candidate and represented Calgary for four years in Ottawa. Religion: united Church. He died in May 1932.

Patrick Harvey Ashby, *Social Credit for Edmonton East 1945-1949*

Born in Sussex, England in 1890, he was the son of Frederick Ashby, a Britisher. He was educated at private schools in England, at Wadham College, Oxford, and at the University of Alberta, he came to Canada at the age of fifteen. Ashby became a successful farmer and rancher in the Edmonton district. He served in the Canadian army during the Great War. He became active in federal politics when he ran as a Social Credit candidate in 1945 for the urban riding of Edmonton East. He won the election and served one term in the Commons. He was an Anglican.

Gerald William Baldwin, *Progressive Conservative for Peace River 1958-Present*

Born at Palmerston, New Zealand in 1907, he was the son of Vaudrey Baldwin, who was of British descent. Coming to Canada as a child with his parents, he was educated at Edmonton and the University of Alberta. He established a legal practice in the Peace River district of northern Alberta. He has been named a Q.C. and a bencher of the Alberta Law Society. He has been interested in politics all his life. He first ran as a Conservative in the provincial election of 1935 which saw William Aberhart's Social Crediters come to power. He was defeated. He ran again as a Conservative federally in 1957 with no better luck. Baldwin was first elected in the Diefenbaker sweep of 1958. He has held the large northern Alberta riding since. In the last federal election, he had a 7000-odd vote majority. He has recently been named House leader of the Conservative group in the House of Commons. He is an Anglican.

Harold Raymond Ballard, *Progressive Conservative for Calgary South 1965-1968*

Born at Provost, Alberta in 1918, he is the son of William Ballard and Mable Armstrong, both of British descent. He was educated at Lloydminster and the University of British Columbia where he received a Bachelor of Arts and a Bachelor of Commerce degree. Ballard is a Calgary chartered accountant. He became interested in civic politics in the 1960s, and served four years as a Calgary alderman (1962-1966) before he moved into federal politics. He was the Progressive Conservative candidate in Calgary South in the 1965 general election. He won the seat by a narrow margin of 155 votes. Three years later, he was defeated by Liberal Patrick Mahoney, who was named to Trudeau's cabinet in 1972 as the Minister of State. He is an Anglican.

Richard Bedford Bennett, *MLA for the NWT 1898-1905; Conservative MLA for Calgary 1909-1911; Conservative for Calgary 1911-1917, 1925-1938; Minister of Justice 1921; Minister of Finance 1926; Prime Minister of Canada 1930-1935; Leader of the Opposition 1935-1938*

Born at Hopewell, New Brunswick in 1870, he was on both his father's and mother's side of the ninth generation born in North America. His father's ancestors were of United Empire Loyalist stock while his mother's people came directly to Canada in 1760. He was educated at public schools in New Brunswick and at Dalhousie University, Halifax, where he obtained a law degree. He was called to the New Brunswick Bar in 1893 and started to practice law in Chatham with L.J. Tweedie as his partner. Senator James Lougheed persuaded him to join his Calgary firm. Bennett, who became a very wealth man and never married, was always interested in politics. He was, during the course of his life, elected to the Regina legislature of the Northwest Territories, the Alberta legislature (1909-1911), and the House of Commons (1911-1917 and 1925-1938). He served in Arthur Meighen's first cabinet in 1921 as Minister of Justice and in his second cabinet in 1925 as Minister of Finance. In 1927, at a convention held in Winnipeg, Bennett was chosen as the leader of the Conservative party; and in the general election of 1930, he led his party to victory. He became Prime Minister, taking over at the same time the portfolios of Finance and External Affairs. His period of office coincided with the most severe years of the depression, and his efforts to counter the effects of economic crisis did not prove successful. His government was voted out of office in the 1935 general election even though he was re-elected again in Calgary. He was the leader of the opposition until he retired from public life in 1938 and went to live in the south of England. In 1941, he was created Viscount Bennett of Michleham, Calgary and Hopewell. He died at Dorking in 1947. His papers are at the University of New Brunswick. (See: Ernest Watkins, R.B. Bennett)

Hilliard Harris Beyerstein, *Social Credit for Camrose 1949-1953*

Born at Meeting Creek, Alberta in 1907, he was the son of Fred Beyerstein and Clara Lindquist, his wife, both of whom were of Swedish descent. He was educated at meeting creek and palmer school of chiropractic, Davenport, Iowa, where he obtained a doctor of chiropractic degree. He established his practice in Camrose and was active in the social credit movement like several other members of his profession. In 1949, he was named the Social Credit candidate in Camrose. He sat in the federal House for one term. In 1953, redistribution eliminated the Camrose riding. He thus retired from politics at the age of forty-five. Religion: Lutheran.

Frederick Jack Bigg, *Progressive Conservative for Athabasca 1958-1968; Progressive Conservative for Pembina 1968-Present*

Born at Meskanaw, Saskatchewan in 1912, he is the son of Frederick Bigg, who was of British descent. He was educated at Prince Albert Coolegiate, the University of Saskatchewan and the University of Toronto, where he obtained a law degree in 1953. As a young man, he joined the Royal Canadian Mounted Police and was a sergeant when he retired from the force. He saw active service with the Royal Canadian Horse Artillery as a captain during the Second World War. He was a lawyer in Westlock when he entered federal politics in 1958 and was elected for the large northern riding of Athabasca. He was re-elected in the 1962, 1963, 1965 and 1968 general elections, the last time for the newly-created riding of Pembina. He is an Anglican.

John Horn Blackmore, *Social Credit for Lethbridge 1935-1958*

Born at Sublett, Idaho, United States in 1890, of British descent, he was educated at Cardston and the university of Alberta, where he obtained a bachelor of arts degree in 1913. He then attended the Calgary normal school. Blackmore married Emily Woolley of Raymond, Alberta, and had a large family. He taught at several schools in southern Alberta before becoming the principal at Raymond in 1921, a position he held for the next fourteen years until he entered federal politics. He was the Social Credit candidate for Lethbridge where he defeated the incumbent, General John Stewart. He held the riding for the next twenty-three years. He served as the social Credit House leader in the Commons from 135-1944. He was mentioned as a possible successor to the deceased William "Bible Bill" Aberhart in 1943, but the Social Credit caucus passed him over to give the job to Ernest Manning.

While in the federal House, he was instrumental in securing federal construction of St. Mary River Dam as well as the Waterton and Belly River dams, the mainstay of Alberta's irrigation projects. He was made an honorary Chief of the Kainai tribe of the Blood Indian Reserve in 1945. His Indian title was "motuskumau" (Wise Counsellor). He is the author of several books on Social Credit theory and was an influential member of the Mormon community.

William John Blair, *Conservative for Battle River 1917-1921*

Born at Embro, Ontario in 1875 of Irish descent, he was educated at Woodstock Collegiate Institute and the School of Practical Science, Toronto (Bachelor of Applied Science). Prior to coming to Alberta, he was a school teacher in Ontario and spent seven years as a mining engineer in Cobalt. He then became the mayor of New Liseard. Ontario, 1907-1908. He came west in 1910, where he became a successful farmer in the Provost district of Alberta. He was defeated three times provincially before he ran federally. He was elected in the general election of 1917 as the Unionist member for Battle River. Blair did not stand for re-election in the 1921 election.

Kenneth Alexander Blatchford, *Liberal for Edmonton East 1926-1930*

Born at Minnedosa, Manitoba in 1881 of British descent, he was educated at Minnedosa and the Commercial College, Winnipeg. He became an insurance broker and was elected an Edmonton alderman in the early 1920s. he served as mayor of Edmonton from 1924 to 1926. He entered federal politics as a Liberal candidate for Edmonton East in the 1926 general election. He defeated the incumbent, Conservative A.U.W. Bury, by a small majority if 165 votes, but was unseated by Bury four years later. Religion: Presbyterian. He died in April of 1933.

Arthur Moren Boutillier, *UFA for Vegreville 1925-1926*

Born at Halifax, Nova Scotia in 1869, he was the son of Esrom Boutillier, French and Anne Spear, his Irish wife. He was educated at the Halifax Academy and came to western Canada as a young man. He was the municipal treasurer of the district of Eagle for many years commencing in 1904. He was active in the UFA movement and entered federal politics in 1925 as the Progressive candidate for the new riding of Vegreville. He was elected with the large majority of 2460 votes. He did not seek re-election in the next federal election held in 1926. In 1940 he attempted to get re-elected in Vegreville. This time he ran as a CCFer, but was among the "also ran". He was an Anglican.

Edwin William (Ted) Brundsen, *Progressive Conservative for Medicine Hat 1958-1962*

Born in Kent, England in 1896, he is the son of Samuel Brunsden. He was educated at Calgary, the Olds Agricultural College and the University of Alberta where he obtained a Bachelor of Science degree. He is an agricultural agent in Brooks, Alberta. As a young man, he saw active service with the 29th infantry battalion in the Great War. Entering federal politics in 1957, he was defeated by then Social Crediter Bud Olson. However, in the Diefenbaker sweep of Alberta in 1958, he was elected. He was defeated again by Olson in the 1962 election, whereupon he retired from active politics. He was an Anglican.

William Ashbury Buchanan, *Liberal for Lethbridge 1911-1921*

Summoned to the Senate in 1925. (See list of Senators)

John Francis Buckley, *Liberal for Athabasca 1930-1931*

Born at Butte, Montana, United States in 1891, he was the son of John Buckley who was of British descent. He came to Canada as a young man in 1911 after being educated in Wales and at the Inner Temple in London, England. He started a law practice in St. Paul, Alberta, before seeing active service with the Princess Patricia's Canadian Light Infantry during the Great War. He entered politics in 1930 when he ran as a Liberal in the large northern riding of Athabasca. He was elected with a 1261 vote majority. He died a year later while still a Member of Parliament. Religion: United Church.

Ambrose Upton Gledstanes Bury, *Conservative for Edmonton East 1925-1926*

Born at Doronings House, Kildare, Ireland in 1869, he was the son of Charles bury, J.P. and Margaret Aylmer, both Anglo-Irish. His mother's family had a long connection with Canada. Matthem, fifth Baron Aylmer, was a Governor-General of Canada during the 1830s and remained in the country. Bury was educated at the Royal School Raphoe, County Donegal, and Trinity College, Dublin University where he received a Master of Arts degree in 1893. He was subsequently called to the Irish Bar as a member of the King's Inns, Dublin, in 1906. He then came to Canada and established a law practice in Edmonton. He was called to the Alberta Bar in 1913 and appointed a King's Councillor in 1928. Always interested in politics, Bury was a Conservative candidate in the 1921 provincial election but failed to get elected. The next year, he successfully ran for the Edmonton city council. He was an alderman from 1922 to 1925. He was elected as a Conservative in the 1925 federal election, but was defeated by Liberal Blatchford the next year. Bury then became the mayor of Edmonton in 1927 and was re-elected in 1928 and 1929. He returned to federal politics in 1930 when he in turn defeated incumbent Blatchford. He retired from politics in 1935 when he reached the age of 66. Bury was appointed a judge of the Northern District Court in 1936. He was an Anglican. He died in March 1951.

Mrs. Cora Taylor Casselman, Liberal for Edmonton East 1941-1945

Born at Tara, Ontario in 1888, she was the daughter of Francis Watt Taylor and Elizabeth Noble, both of British descent. She was educated at Toronto Public School and Queen's University where she obtained a Bachelor of Arts degree. She married Frederick C. Casselman, K.C., an Edmonton lawyer in 1916. Mrs.

Casselman was active in a number of organizations including University Women's Club, Council of Social Agencies and the Community Chest. She was elected in 1941 in a by-election caused by the death of her husband. She increased the Liberal minority in a three-way struggle. Her opponents were Macleod for the Conservatives and Orvis Kennedy, Social Credit, who had held the urban riding from 1938 to 1940. Mrs. Casselman is the only woman ever to be elected to represent an Alberta constituency in the federal Parliament. She died in September 1964.

Frederick Clayton Casselman, *Liberal for Edmonton East 1940-1941*

Born at Helmsville, Montana, United States in 1885, he was the son of Samuel Casselman and Albertina Hillborn, both Canadians. His parents returned to Canada when he was a child of five years. He was educated at Forest and Watford High School, Queen's University (B.A.) and the University Of Ontario (LL.B). Casselman married in 1916 Cora Taylor, daughter of Francis Watt Taylor of Barrie, Ontario. They had one daughter. He saw active service as a sergeant in the Canadian Expeditionary Force in France during the Great War. In 1918, he was commissioned into the Wiltshire regiment. On his return to Canada, he established a legal practice in Edmonton where he became active in civic affairs. He was elected to the Edmonton Public School Board in 1928, and served on it for the next nine years. In 1927, he was elected an alderman and three years later ran against incumbent SoCred Orvis Kennedy in Edmonton East. He was successful in his first attempt to enter the federal House. However, he died within the year. His widow, Cora Casselman, ran also as a Liberal in the resulting by-election. She was victorious and thus became the only woman Alberta has ever sent to Ottawa as Member of Parliament.

Douglas Marmaduke Caston, *Progressive Conservative for Jasper-Edson 1967-1968*

Born at Macklin, Saskatchewan in 1917, he is the son of John E. Caston and Edna Walker, both Canadians of British descent. He was educated at Macklin and took a war-time course in law at Oxford. He is the publisher of the Edson newspaper and president of the Yellowhead Press. He saw active service in the Second World War in Europe in the Canadian Air Force. Caston was first elected to the Commons in a by-election caused when Dr. Hugh Horner resigned is federal seat in order to run provincially in 1967. His majority was 2861 votes. The riding of Jasper-Edson disappeared in the redistribution prior to the 1968 federal election. Caston failed to obtain the official Progressive Conservative nomination in the newly-created riding of Rocky Mountain. However, he ran as an Independent Conservative, splitting the anti-government vote which enable Liberal Allen Sulatycky to take the seat. Caston ran third in a way six-way contest. He is an Anglican.

Dr. Michael Clark, *Liberal for Red Deer 1908-1921*

Born at Bedford, Northumberland, England in 1861, he was educated at Elmfield College, York and Edinburgh University where he obtained M.B. and C.M. degrees. He was a member of the Newcastle-on-tyne School Board before he came to Canada. He was one of the two Liberal candidates who didn't secure election to the formal Legislature of 1905. He was defeated by the conservative candidate, Cornelius Hiebert, a Mennonite of Russian birth in the constituency of Rosebud. In 1908, he was elected to the Commons for the newly0created riding of Red Deer and held the seat for the next thirteen years. Dr. Clark was one of the most influential Liberals in Alberta, and was the first to commit himself to support conscription and to oppose Laurier. He ran in thr 1917 federal election as a Unionist candidate, but because of failing health did not get named to Borden's cabinet. Instead, Premier Arthur Sifton resigned his seat in the Legislature to enter the federal cabinet as Minister of the Interior. He was again an official Liberal candidate in 1921 for MacKenzie, Saskatchewan, but was defeated. In his service in the Commons, Dr. Clark won renown as powerful orator, an uncanny skillful rhetorician and a master of refined and telling English. He won the soubriquet of "Red Michael" which clung to him throughout his career. He died in July 1926, at Olds, Alberta.

George Gibson Coote, *UFA for Macleod 1921-1935*

Born at Oakville, Ontario in 1880, and educated there, he came to Alberta as young man and married Jennet

McKinnon of Nanton in 1910. As a successful farmer in the Nanton district, he was active in UFA affairs and was swept to power in 19921. He held the seat until the UFA was unseated by the Social Credit in 1935. He had run that year as a CCF candidate. In 1936, Coote was named a director of the Bank of Canada, he died in November 1958. He was a Methodist.

Charles Wilson Cross, *Liberal for Athabasca 1925-1926; MLA for Edson 1905-1025; Alberta Attorney-General 1905-1910, 1913-1918*

Born at Madoc, Ontario in 1872, he was the son of Thomas Cross, who was of British descent. He was educated at Upper Canada College, the University of Toronto (B.A. 1895) and Osgoode Hall (LL.B. 1896). Becoming a lawyer in 1898, he established his law practice in Edmonton. He entered provincial politics in 1905 when he was elected for the constituency of Edson. He sat continuously in the Legislature for the next twenty years and was one of the most influential Liberals in Alberta. He was named Attorney-General in Rutherford's first administration. He resigned this portfolio in 1910. Premier Sifton re-appointed him Attorney-General in 1913. He held the post for five years. In 1921, Cross was one of the two members who had been elected in 1905 to withstand the United Farmers of Alberta sweeping victory. At this time, *the Montreal Star* said that Cross was "regarded as a coming man". He entered federal politics in 1925 when he won the newly created Athabasca riding.

However, he was defeated at UFA Kellner the next year. Religion: Presbyterian. He died in June, 1928 at Calgary.

Colonel Douglas G.L. Cunnington, *M.C., Conservative for Calgary West 1939-1940*

Born at Bridgenorth, England in 1885, he was the son of a school master, educated at the Blue Coat School, Bridgenorth, he came to Canada as a young man and settled in Calgary in 1910. Prior to this, he had spent five years in British Guiana. He owned and operated a large dairy near the city. In 1915, he enlisted as a private in the Canadian Army, but was soon commissioned. He was awarded the Military Cross "for conspicuous gallantry in front of Hallu, France," in August 1918. He led his platoon forward to capture a German machine-gun nest. The following day he was shot through the chest and left for dead in No Man's Land. His comrades reported killed in action, but a few hours later, a German ambulance crew took him to a German military hospital. It was not until several weeks later that his wife was informed he was still alive. On his return to Calgary, he worked for The Calgary Herald for several years before becoming an insurance broker. He was always interested in politics. He served on the Calgary city council for six years commencing in 1934. When former Prime Minister R.B. Bennett resigned his seat in the Commons in order to take up permanent residence in the United Kingdom, Cunnington was elected by acclamation to Parliament for the Calgary West riding.

However, he was defeated when he sought re-election in 1940.

Percy Griffith Davies, *Conservative for Athabasca 1932-1935*

Born at Edmonton in 1902, he was the son of Arthur Davies and Mary Parry, both of British descent. His father was mayor of Strathcona for several years. He was educated at Strathcona High School and the University of Alberta where he obtained a Bachelor of Arts and a Law degree. While at the University, he became the secretary-treasurer of the national federation of Canadian University students and the president of the students' union. He established a law practice at Clyde, Alberta, and entered federal politics as a Conservative in 1932 in a by-election caused by the death of Liberal John Buckley, MP for Athabasca. He had a narrow victory margin of 324 votes. He was under thirty years of age when he was first elected to the Commons. He was not a candidate three years later when Alberta went Social Credit. Religion: United Church.

Donald Watson Davis, *Conservative for Alberta, N.W.T. 1887-1896*

He was born in Londenderry, Vermont in 1848 of British descent. He was educated there and settled in the Macleod district of the \northwest Territories about 1870. Davis became a successful merchant and general stik dealer in Macleod. He was first elected to the House of commons in 1887 and had the honor of being the first elected representative from the Northwest Territories to sit in Parliament. He was the sole member of the House for the next nine years, sitting on the Conservative side of the House. He was not a candidate in the general election of 1896 that saw Wilfrid Laurier become the Prime Minister of Canada. He died in June 1906.

Frederick Davis, *Conservative for Calgary East 1925-1926*

Born at Mitchell, Ontario in 1868, he was the son of W.R. Davis, who was of British descent. His father was editor and proprietor of a weekly newspaper, The Mitchell Advocate, for some fifty-eight years. Davis was elected councilor, reeve and mayor of his home town before he came to Alberta. He homesteaded in the Irricana district and in time became a successful farmer. Je was always interested in politics. He ran provincially in the 1917 general election as Independent Conservative for the Gleichen constituency. He was the winner in a three-way contest and sat in the Legislature for the next four years. He entered federal politics in 1925 and was elected in Calgary East. He was not able to hold the seat in the next general election held a year later. Religion: Anglican.

Joseph Miville Dechene, *Liberal for Athabasca 1940-1958*

Born at Chambord, Quebec in 1879, he was the son of Leon Dechene, whose ancestors had come to New

France in 1623. He was educated at Roberval and at Quebec Seminary. Dechene married Maria, granddaughter of Wilfrid Gariepy, an influential member of the provincial cabinets of Arthur Sifton and Charles Stewart. Senator J.P. Lessard (see: Senators) was also a relation of his wife. He farmed for many years in the Bonnyville district of northeastern Alberta and entered provincial politics as the Liberal candidate for Beaver River in 1921, replacing W. Garieoy there. After one term in the Legislature, he entered civil politics in Bonnyville, where he was councilor from 1928 to 1934. In 1940, he entered federal politics as the Liberal candidate for Athabasca which he represented for the next eighteen years. His fellow MP from Peace River, John Sissons, considered him one of the smartest politicians Alberta ever produced. When he ran for the last time in 1957, Dechene was the oldest member of the House of Commons, being seventy-eight years of age. His margin of victory over SoCred Archie McPhail had been only 424. He did not seek re-election in the general election held the next spring. He was a prominent Roman Catholic. His son, Andre Dechene, is a justice of the Supreme Court of Alberta. He died in December 1962, at Edmonton.

John Decore, *Liberal for Vegreville 1949-1957*

Born at Andrew, Alberta in 1909 of Ukrainian descent, he was educated at Andrew, Edmonton, and at the University of Alberta where he obtained a B.A. and L.L.B. while he was qualifying himself with a lawyer, he taught in the Vegreville High School. He established his law practice in Edmonton and Vegreville. He entered federal politics in 1949 when he stood for the Vegreville riding. He won the seat and was re-elected four years later. He did not stand in 1957. Decore was named a Q.C. in 1964. He is now a judge of the District Court of northern Alberta. Religion: Greek Orthodox.

John McCrie Douglas, *Liberal for Strathcona 1909-1921*

Born at Middleville, Ontario in 1867, he was the son of Rev. James Douglas of British descent. He received his education at Morris, Manitoba. As a young man he came west to Edmonton in 1894and then to Strathcona, across the river from Edmonton where he established himself as a merchant in 1901. He was a member of the Strathcona city council for two years. Entering federal politics in 1909, he ran as the Liberal candidate in a by-election caused by the death of the sitting member, Dr. Wilbert McIntyre, and was elected by acclamation. He held the constituency for the next twelve years. Douglas was defeated in 1921 when he ran as a Conservative candidate. Religion: Presbyterian.

Cliff Downey, *Progressive Conservative for Battle River 1968-Present*

First elected to the House of Commons in the 1968 general election, he had one of the largest majorities in Canada totaling 11,603 votes. Tory farmer Cliff

Smallwood had previously held the constituency since the Diefenbaker sweep of 1958. In April 1972, Harry M. Kuntz, a forty-three-year-old Cmarose alderman, won the Progressive Conservative nomination for the forthcoming election.

Manley Justin Edwards, *Liberal for Calgary West 1940-1945*

Born at Caistorville, Ontario in 1892, he was educated at Hamilton, Ontario, Calgary normal school, and the University of Alberta (LL.B.). He taught in Alberta schools while getting his law degree. He established his law practice in Calgary and was active for years in service clubs. He was a national president of Kinsmen Clubs of Canada. He was a Calgary alderman from 1929 to 1950. Edwards ran against incumbent Conservative D.G.L. Cunnington in Calgary West in the 1940 election. He was successful in capturing R.B. Bennett's old seat. He only spent one term in the federal House. He was appointed a judge of the southern Alberta District Court in 1950. Religion: United Church. Edwards died while still a judge in May 1962 at Calgary.

Robert Fair, *Social Credit for Battle River 1935-1954*

Born at Keelognes, Ireland in 1891, he was educated there before he came to Canada in 1914. Fair married in 1919 the daughter of C.S. Holmstrom of Paradise Valley, Alberta. He was a farmer in the Paradise Valley district. First elected to the Commons as a Social Crediter in 1935 for the rural riding of Battle

River, he held the seat until his death some twenty years later in November 1954. Religion: United Church.

Frank John William Fane, *Progressive Conservative for Vegreville 1958-1968*

Born at Beaver Lake, Alberta in 1897, he is the son of Frank W. Fane and Margaret Duff, both of British descent. His father had been an unsuccessful Conservative candidate for the Victoria constituency in 1905 and 1909. He was educated at Beaver Lake, Vegreville, Camrose normal school and the service in the Canadian Expeditionary Force during the Great War. On his return from overseas, he became a farmer in the Mundare district. He was active for many years in municipal affairs, serving both on the municipal board and the school board. He was an unsuccessful Conservative candidate for the Vegreville riding in 1940 and again in 1957. He was first elected at the age of sixty-one in 1958 when all seventeen Alberta ridings went Conservative. He was re-elected in 1962, 1963, and 1965. He retired in 1968. He is an Anglican.

Robert Gardiner, *UFA for Medicine Hat 1921-1925; UFA for Acadia 1925-1935*

Born in Aberdeenshire, Scotland I 179, he came to Canada in 1902 after being educated in Scotland. Councillor and Reeve of the municipal district of Golden Centre, Alberta, from 1914 to 1921, he was first elected to the Commons in a by-election caused by the death of Arthur Sifton in 1921. He was reelected in 1925, 1926, and 1930, but was defeated in 1935. Gardiner had been elected the UFA president in 1931 when Henry Wise Wood had retired. He died in February 1945 at Calgary. Gardiner never married. Religion: Presbyterian.

Edward Joseph Garland, *UFA for Bow River 1921-1935*

Born at Dublin, Ireland in 1995, he came to Canada in 1909. He was educated at Belvidera College and Trinity College, Dublin University. He left before he obtained a degree. He became a farmer in the Ramsey district of central Alberta. He became active in the United Farmers of Alberta movement, being an executive officer of the farm organization in 1921. He represented Bow River riding in Ottawa from 1921 ti 1935. He was defeated by Social Crediter Charles Johnston in 1935. He was a Roman Catholic.

Dr. Frederick Gershaw, *Liberal for Medicine Hat 1925-1935 and 1940-1945*

Senator from Alberta 1945-1963

(See: List of Senators)

General William Antrobus Griesbach, *Conservative for Edmonton West 1917-1921*

Senator from Alberta 1921-1944

(See: List of Senators)

Deane Roscoe Gundlock, *Progressive Conservative for Lethbridge 1948-Present*

Born at Warner, Alberta in 1914, he is the son of Emil Herman Gundlock, British, and Arline Huilt, American. He was educated at West Denver. He is a successful farmer and partner in an import/export company. He has served on the local school board (1946-1948), and the Warner municipal council (1946-1958) before entering federal politics in 1948. He was elected for Lethbridge and held the seat in the next four general elections. In January 1972, he announced that he would not be seeking re-election, but would retire from politics. Religion: Protestant.

Dr. William Samuel Hall, *Social Credit for Edmonton East 1935-1938*

Born at Mount Forrests, Ontario in 1871, he was the son of William Hall and Mary Gillies, his wife, both Canadians. He was educated at Hawkesbury, Ontario, and Royal College of Dental Surgeons and the University of Toronto where he obtained L.D.S. and D.D.S. degrees. He came to Edmonton to establish his dental practice. Dr. Hall was an admirer of William Aberhart and ran as a Social Credit candidate in the 1935 provincial election. He was defeated at the polls, but obtained the SoCred nomination for Edmonton East riding and was elected to the Commons in the federal election held later that year. He was sixty-six years of age at the time. He died two years later while still a sitting Member of Parliament. Orvis Kennedy held the seat for the

Social Credit in the resulting by-election. Religion: Baptist.

Howard Hadden Halladay, *Unionist for Bow River 1917-1921*

Born at Elgin, Ontario in 1878, he was educated at Athens, Ontario and Winnipeg. He came west and became an insurance agent and farmer. He was mayor of Hanna, Alberta, from 1913 to 1918. He was first elected to the Commons as a Unionist in the 1917 general election. He was not a candidate in the 1921 federal election. Religion: Methodist.

R.F.L. "Dick" Hanna, *Liberal for Edmonton Strathcona 1953-1957*

Born at Monaghan, Ireland in 1913, he was educated at Mountjoy School, Dublin, Drumheller, Calgary normal school and the University of Alberta where he obtained a Bachelor of Arts degree. He taught school in Alberta during the 1930s before seeing active service in the RCAF during the Second World War. He worked for the Veterans Land Act administration after leaving the armed services. He entered civic politics in 1948 when he was elected as an Edmonton alderman. He was on the city council for five years. In the 1953 general election, he ran as Liberal candidate in an urban riding. He won the seat by 151 votes. His nearest rival was Orvis Kennedy, president of the Social Credit League and a former Member of Parliament. He failed in his re-election bid, being defeated by SoCred Syd Thompson. He is now an insurance salesman. Religion: United Church.

Rev. Ernest George Hansell, **Social Credit for Macleod 1935-1958**

Born at Norwich, England in 1895, he came to Canada at the age of nine. Educated at the Bible Institute of Los Angeles and the Southern Divinity School, Dallas, Texas, he became a minister of the Christian Church in Vulcan and was a special lecturer at the Alberta Bible College. He entered politics in 1935 and represented the southern Alberta riding of Macleod in Ottawa for the net twenty-three years. He was defeated in 1958 by Progressive Conservative Dr. Kindt. Hansell then entered provincial politics and was the Member of the Legislature for Okotoks-High River from 1959 to 1963. He retired at sixty-eight years of age. Hansell died in December of 1965, at Calgary.

Douglas Harkness, *Progressive Conservative for Calgary North 1945-1068; Progressive Conservative for Calgary Centre 1968-Present; Minister of Northern Affairs, 1957-1958; Minister of Agriculture 1957-1960; Minister of National Defence, 1960-1963*

Born at Toronto in 1903, he was the son of William Harkness and Janet Scott, both of British descent. He was educated at Calgary central Collegiate and the University of Alberta where he obtained a Bachelor's degree. He first became a high school teacher and later a farmer. During the Second World War,

Harkness saw active service in Sicily, Italy, and northwest Europe as an artillery officer. He was first elected to the House of Commons in 1945 and has been re-elected a total of eight times as one of the Members for the city of Calgary. He is at present the dean in length of service in Parliament among Alberta's representatives in Ottawa. Harkness was named to Diefenbaker's first cabinet in 1957 as Minister of Northern Affairs and National Resources. A few weeks later, he was appointed Minister of Agriculture, a post he held for the next three years. In 1960, the fifty-seven year old former artillery colonel was transferred to the Department of National Defence. He was the Minister of National Defense until early 1963, when he quit the federal cabinet due to a policy disagreement with Diefenbaker. In early 1972, he announced that he would not seek re-election in the forthcoming federal election. Religion: Presbyterian.

Dr. Hu Harris, *Liberal for Edmonton Stratchcona, 1968-Present*

Born at Strathmore, Alberta in 1921, of British descent, he was educated at the University of Alberta, University of Toronto, and Iowa State University (Ph.D. degree). He served from 1953 to 1959 as an Edmonton alderman. He was on the faculty of the University of Alberta when he was first elected to the House of Commons in 1968. He refers to himself as an economist. Religion: United Church.

William Hayhurst, *Social Credit for Vegreville, 1935-1940*

Born at Lyvennet Mill, Morland, England in 1887, he was the son of Gilbert Hayhurst and Sara Burrow, both British. He was educated at Morland and Appleby grammar school before coming to Canada in 1910. He later attended the University of Alberta. Hayhurst was for years the principal of the Vegreville High School. He was also the reeve of Minburn from 1923-1924. He first ran federally in 1930 but was defeated. In 1935 he tried again, this time as a Social Crediter, and was successful. He retired from politics after only serving one term in the federal House. Religion: United Church.

Harry William Hays, *Liberal for Calgary South 1963-1965*

Minister of Agriculture 1963-1965

Senator from Alberta 1966-Present

(See: List of Senators)

John Herron, Conservative for Alberta 1904-1908; Conservative for Macleod 1908-1911

Born at Ashton, Carleton County, Ontario in 1853, he was educated at Ashton public schools. He came west into the Northwest Territories as a young man, an original member of the N.W.M.P and helped establish Fort Macleod in 1874 and Fort Calgary in 1875. He then became a successful rancher in the

Pincher Creek district of southern Alberta. He was a license commissioner and stock inspector in the province. Herron raised a company of Rocky Mountain Rangers and served during the North West Rebellion, 1885. He was first elected to the Commons in 1904 by a 78-vote majority. His Liberal opponent was Malcolm Mackenzie. He was re-elected in 1908. He was defeated in 1911. Herron died in August 1936, at Pincher Creek. Religion: Presbyterian.

Anthony Hlynka, *Social Credit for Vegreville 1940-1949*

Born in the Western Ukraine in 1907, he came to Canada with his parents when he was still a child. He was educated in Delph and Edmonton and attended the technical school in Edmonton. He worked as a journalist and was a publisher of a weekly newspaper. He entered federal politics in 1940 and won the Vegreville riding for the Social Credit movement. He was re-elected five years later but failed to hold the seat in 1949 when he was opposed by Liberal lawyer John Decore. He is a member of the Greek Orthodox Church.

Ambrose Holowach, *Social Credit for Edmonton East 1953-1958*

Born at Edmonton in 1914, he was the son of Sam Holowach and Josephine Dwornik, both Ukrainians. He was educated at Edmonton and studied music in Europe, supporting himself by writing on music festivals. During the Second World War, he served with the Canadian signal corps. He owned and operated the family dry-cleaning firm. He failed in 1949 in his first bid to get into Parliament but was successful four years later in the urban riding of Edmonton East. He lost his seat in the Diefenbaker landslide of 1958. However, the next year he entered provincial politics. He represented an Edmonton constituency in the Legislature for the next twelve years until he was unseated by the Lougheed sweep of 1971. In 1962, he was appointed Provincial Secretary and was chairman of the Alberta Centennial Committee in 1967 s well as being the province's representative on the National Centennial Committee. Holowach was defeated in the 1971 provincial election by Dave King and retired from politics. He is a Ukrainian Catholic.

Dr. Hugh MacArthur Horner, *Progressive Conservative for Jasper-Edson 1958-1967*

Born at Blaine Lake, Saskatchewan in 1925, he is the son of the late Senator Ralph Horner and brother to jack Horner, Conservative MP for Crowfoot. He was educated at Blaine Lake, University of Saskatchewan (B.A.) and the University of Western Ontario (M.D.). Upon obtaining his medical degree, he established a practice at Barrhead, Alberta. He was first elected to the Commons in the 1958 election for the Jasper-Edson riding. He resigned his seat in 1967 in order to enter provincial politics. He was one of the small groups of Conservatives elected to the Legislature in 1967. He was re-elected in 1971 and was named to

Lougheed's cabinet as Deputy Premier and Minister of Agriculture. Religion: United Church.

John Henry Horner, *Progressive Conservative for Acadia 1958-1968; Progressive Conservative for Crowfoot 1968-Present*

Born at Blaine Lake, Saskatchewan in 1927, he is the son of the late Senator Ralph Horner and younger brother of Dr. Hugh Horner, Deputy Premier of Alberta and Minster of Agriculture in the Lougheed cabinet. He was educated at the University of Alberta and is a successful rancher in the Pollockville district of Alberta. He entered federal politics in 1958 when he was elected the Tory Member of Parliament for Acadia. This riding disappeared in the 1968 redistribution, but Horner was elected for the newly-created riding of Crowfoot. He is one of the most colorful members in the federal House from Alberta. Religion: United Church.

William Irvine, *Labor for Calgary East 1921-1925; UFA for Wetaskiwin 1926-1935*

Born in the Shetland Islands, Scotland in 1885, he came to Canada as a youth in 1902. He was educated at Manitoba and Wesley Colleges, Winnipeg. Irvine was a Presbyterian Minister at Emo, Ontario 1913-1915, and a Unitarian clergyman at Calgary 1915-1919. He was acquitted in ecclesiastical courts of the charge of heresy in 1914. The author of several pamphlets and plays, he was editor of the Western Farmer and the People's Weekly. After the

Great War, he homesteaded in the Bentley district. He became a successful farmer. He was active in politics all his life, running unsuccessfully both provincially and federally in 1917. He was first elected to Parliament as a Labor candidate in Calgary East in 1921. He failed to hold the seat in the 1925 general election, but was successful in Wetaskiwin as UFA candidate the next year, which he represented in Ottawa for nine years. Irvine was active in the CCF party for many years. He was elected for the federal riding of Cariboo in 1945 but was defeated again four years later. Irvine died in October 1962 at Edmonton. Religion: Unitarian.

Norman Jaques, *Social Credit for Wetaskiwin 1935-1949*

Born at London, England in 1880, he was educated at Eastbourne College prior to coming to Canada as a young man in 1901. Jaques homesteaded in the Mirror district of Alberta, becoming a successful farmer. He entered federal politics in 1935, winning the rural riding of Wetaskiwin. He represented this constituency for the next fourteen years in Ottawa. He died while still a Member in January 1949. He was an Anglican.

Lincoln Henry Jelliff, *Progressive for Lethbridge 1921-1930*

Born at Oneida, Illinois, United States in 1865, he was the son of Fletcher Jelliff whose ancestors came to America from Britain in colonial days. He was educated at Oneida and Know College, Galesburg, where he obtained an M.A. degree. He came to Canada in 1902 to homestead in the Raley district. Jelliff was a successful farmer. He successfully ran for the House of Commons in 1921 as a Progressive. He was re-elected in 1925 and 1926 but was defeated by Tory general John Stewart in the 1930 federal election;. Religion: Congregationalist.

Charles Edward Johnston, *Social Credit for Bow River 1935-1958*

Born at Bay Mills, Michigan in 1899, he was the son of Alfred Johnston, a Canadian, and Mary Burgett, his American wife. Coming to Canada while still a child in 1906, he was educated at the University of Alberta, then became a school teacher at the Three Hills district. He was first elected to Parliament in 1935 as a Social Crediter. He was re-elected five times before being defeated by Conservative Eldon Woolliams in 1958. Johnston then entered provincial politics and sat for two terms as the Social Credit member for Calgary – Browness. He retired from politics in 1967 at the age of 68. Johnston died in December 1971, while on holiday in Houston, Texas. Religion: United Church.

Donald Ferdinand Kellner, *Progressive for Edmonton East 1921-1925; UFA for Athabasca 1926-1930*

Born in 1879 at Ethel, Ontario, he was the son of Joseph Kellner, Canadian and Catherine Forsyth, his

Scottish wife. He was educated at the public schools and at Listowel High School before becoming a farmer. He was first elected to Parliament for Edmonton East in 1921. He was defeated in 1925 in his first attempt to represent the large northern rural riding of Athabasca. However, Kellner was successful in the federal election held a year later, running this time as a UFA candidate. He died in April, 1935 in Edmonton. Religion: Presbyterian.

Donald Macbeth Kennedy, *UFA for Edmonton West 1921-1925; UFA for Peace River 1925-1935*

Born at Ballinlaig, Perthshire, Scotland in 1884, he came to Canada as a young man in 1903. He was educated in Scotland and at Brandon College, Manitoba. He homesteaded at the Waterhole district in Alberta, and in time became a successful farmer. He became active in local politics serving as a municipal councilor, and in the United Farmers of Alberta Organization. Kennedy was elected to the provincial riding of Peace River in 1921, but resigned to enter federal politics. He ran in Edmonton west in the 1921 federal election and won. Four years later, he changed constituency and was successful in his bid to be the Peace River representative in Ottawa. He was re-elected in 1926 and again in 1930, but failed to hold the riding against his social credit opponent in 1935. Religion: Baptist.

Orvis Kennedy, *Social Credit for Edmonton East 1938-1940*

Born at Dryden, Ontario in 1907, he was of British descent. He was educated there and at Lafine, Alberta. He became a hardware salesman in Edmonton. He became active in politics as a Social Crediter and was an early supporter of William Aberhart, whom he knew through his association with the Prophetic Bible Institute. He was a provincial candidate in the 1935 election for the multi-member Edmonton constituency. After the first count he was the sixth in a field of twenty-seven candidates for the six-member constituency. However, he failed to hold his position in the re-counts, being narrowly defeated. Three years later, on the death of Dr. Hall, Social Credit Member of Parliament for for Edmonton East, he entered federal politics. He had been Hall's official agent in 1935. It was the first by-election in the province since the Social Credit sweep three years before. He won the three-way struggle, defeating Conservative Walter Cleverey and Liberal Robert Marshall. The night of the by-election Premier Aberhart danced on "Irish jig" when it was known that the Social Credit party had held the riding. Kennedy failed in his re-election bid in 1940 when the seat was captured by Conservative lawyer Frederick Casselman. He then became the president of the social Credit League and chief party organizer. For the next years, he was the organizer of victory for Premier Manning in seven provincial general elections.

Dr. Lawrence Elliott Kindt, *Progressive Conservative for Macleod 1958-1968*

Born at Kiona, State of Washington in 1901, his father homestead in the Nanton district in 1904. He was educated at Nanton and the University of Alberta (B.Sc. 1927); University of Minnesota (M.A. 1930); and the American University, Washington D.C. (Ph.D. 1940). He was a director in his own economic consulting firm in Calgary as well as being a federal agricultural economist. He entered federal politics as a Conservative in 1958 and was elected for the rural riding of Macleod. Kindt held the constituency until he retired undefeated in 1968. Religion: United Church.

Walter Frederick Kuhl, *Social Credit for Jasper-Edson 1935-1949*

Born at Spruce Grove, Alberta in 1905, he was the son of Albert Kuhl, Canadian, and Elisa Schultz, his American wife. Educated at Edmonton and at the Camrose normal school, he was a school teacher at Spruce Grove until he entered federal politics as a Social Credit candidate in the 1935 election. He won the newly-created Jasper-Edson constituency. He was re-elected by a mere eighty votes in 1940. Kuhl held the seat until 1949 when it was captured by the Liberals. Religion: Maravian Brethren.

Marcel Lambert, *Progressive Conservative for Edmonton West 1957-Present, Speaker of the house of Commons 1962-1963; Minister of Veteran Affairs 1963*

Born at Edmonton in 1919, he was the son of J.E. Lambert (Canadian) and Marie Kiwit (Belgian). His grandfather, L.J.A. Lambert, had represented the constituency of St. Albert in the Northwest Territories Legislature in Regina from 1901 to 1905. He was educated at the University of Alberta and was named a Rhodes Scholar, which permitted him to obtain a law degree from Oxford. As a young man he briefly worked in a bank in Morinville, Alberta, before joining the Canadian army during the Second World War. He took part in the ill-fated Dieppe raid in the summer of 1943 and was taken prisoner by the Germans and spent the remainder of the war in a POW camp. On his return into Canada, Lambert attended the University of Alberta where he obtained a Bachelor of Commerce degree in 1947. He was named a Rhodes Scholar the same year, and studied civil law at Oxford. After articling with Emery Jamieson of Edmonton, he was called to the Alberta Bar in 1951. Always very interested in politics, he attempted to get elected to the Legislature in 1952 for the multi-member Edmonton constituency, but was defeated. He was, however, successful in his first bid to get into the Commons in the 1957 general election. He has represented Edmonton West at Ottawa since. In the 1958 election he had a 22,393 vote majority over his nearest rival, Liberal Henry Dyde, who also was a Rhodes Scholar. In 1962 Lambert was elected Speaker of the House of Commons, and for a few weeks in the spring of 1963 he was in Diefenbaker's cabinet as Minster of Veteran Affairs. At present he is the Conservative's chief financial critic. He is a Roman Catholic.

John Charles Landeryou, *Social Credit for Calgary East 1935-1940*

Born at Harriston, Ontario in 1905, he was of British descent. He was educated at Calgary and the Business College, St. Louis, Missouri, before becoming a chef in Calgary. He entered federal politics as a Social Crediter in the 1935 federal election and won the Calgary East constituency. He was defeated in his bid to hold the seat five years later by a narrow 485 vote margin. The victor in this election was G.H. Ross, who later became a Senator. Landeryou then moved to Lethbridge where he was an insurance agent. He entered provincial politics in the 1944 general election and became Lethbridge's representative in the Legislature. During the twenty-seven years he was an MLA, Landeryou took a backseat. Both he and R.S. Lee, MLA for Taber, were expelled from the Social Credit movement in 1955 as a result of a scandal. However, both were re-elected with increased majorities in the general election that year, and were re-admitted into the party. He retired from politics in 1971 at the age of sixty-six. His election machine, however, was able to elect two Social Crediters in the 1971 provincial election that saw the defeat of the Social Credit administration after being in office thirty-six years. Religion: Baptist.

Solon Earl Low, *Social Credit for Peace River 1945-1958*

National Leader of the Social Credit Movement 1945-1958, he was born at Cardston, Alberta in 1900. Son of James Low (Scotch) who was a university graduate, educator and businessman and a member of the constitutional convention of the State of Utah in the 1880s. Low was educated at Cardston; Calgary normal school; University of Alberta; and University of Southern California. He was a well-known high school principal at Stirling when he entered provincial politics in 1935 as a Social Crediter. He was elected for the riding of Warner and was named to Aberhart's cabinet as the Provincial Treasurer in 1937. He was defeated in the 1940 general election, but he was returned by acclamation in Vegreville the same year when the sitting member, George Woytkiw, resigned. His name as mentioned as a possible successor to William Aberhart when he died in 1943. Low remained the Provincial Treasurer until 1944. He was also the Minister of education from 1943 to 1944. He resigned his seat in the Legislature in 1945 to enter federal politics after being named the national leader of the Social Credit movement. He represented the large Peace River constituency in Ottawa for the next thirteen years before becoming a victim of the Diefenbaker sweep in 1958. Low, after twenty-three years of active politics, returned to the classroom in his old school in southern Alberta. He was later named a magistrate by Premier Manning. He died in

1961. He was a prominent member of the Mormon Church.

William Thomas Lucas, *UFA for Camrose 1925-1930*

Born at Baileboro, Ontario in 1875, he was of British descent. Educated at Baileboro and at the Ontario Agricultural College, Guelph, he was a farmer in the Lougheed district of Alberta. He became active in the United Farmers of Alberta movement and ran as a Progressive in the constituency of Victoria in 1921 and was elected by a more than 9600 vote majority. Four years later, Lucas was successful in his re-election bid in the newly created riding of Camrose which he held for the next ten years as a UFA member. He was an Anglican.

Michael Luchkovich, *UFA for Vegreville 1926-1930*

Born 1892 at Shamoka, Pennsylvania, United States, he was of Ukrainian descent. He came to Canada as a youth in 1907 and attended the University of Manitoba where he received a Bachelor of Arts degree. He then became a teacher at Vegreville. Luchkovich entered federal politics when he ran as a UFA candidate in the constituency of Vegreville which he won with a narrow majority. He belonged to the Greek Catholic Church. (See: Michael Luchkovich, *A Ukrainian Canadian in Parliament 1965*)

Albert Frederick MacDonald, *Liberal for Edmonton East 1949-1953*

Born at Winnipeg in 1901, he wast the son of Albert MacDonald and Margaret Veitch, both of British descent. He was educated at Winnipeg's Wesley College./ he was a Candian National Railway employee and active in the trade union movement. He had seen active service wth the Edmonton fusiliers during the Second World War. In 1949, he entered federal politics when he ran as the Liberal candidate in Edmonton East. He was elected and represented this urban riding for one term in the Commons. He failed in his re-election bid in 1953, being defeated by Social Crediter Ambrose Holowach. Religion: Presbyterian.

Henry Arthur Mackie, *Unionist for Edmonton East 1917-1921*

Born at Cookshire, Quebec, in 1878, he was the son of Joseph Ignatius Mackie and Clothilde Lantangue. He was educated at Bishop's University (B.A.) and McGill University before coming to western Canada wher he established a law practice in Edmonton. He was named a K.C. in 1921. Mackie entered federal politics as a Unionist in 1917 and won the urban riding of Edmonton East. He was defeated in the 1921 election. He died in November, 1945, at Edmonton.

James Angus McKinnon, *Liberal for Edmonton West 1935-1949; Minister without Portfolio 1939-1940; Minister of Trade and Commerce 1940-1948;*

Minister of Fisheries 1949; Minister of Mines and Resources 1949; Summoned to the Senate 1949; Minister without Portfolio 1949-1950

(See: List of Senators)

Charles Alexander Magrath, *Conservative for Medicine Hat 1908-1911*

Born at North Augusta, Upper Canada in 1860, he was of British descent. Educated privately, he came west to the Northwest Territories as a young man. He worked there as a land surveyor and irrigation engineer until 1885, when he joined the Gait interests in various enterprises. He was the first mayor of the town of Lethbridge. He sat for Lethbridge in the Regina Parliament from 1891 to 1902, serving as Minister without Portfolio in the Haultain cabinet, 1898-1901. Entering federal politics as a Conservative, he represented Medicine Hat in the Commons from 1908 to 1911. Magrath was defeated in 1911 by the young publisher of The Lethbridge Herald, W.A. Buchanan. In the years that followed he acted on many boards and advisory committees. Magrath was the author of *Canada's Growth and Some Problems Affecting It (1910)* and of historical articles on the Canadian west. Magrath married for the first time in 1887 Margaret Holmes Mair, who was the daughter of Charles Mair of the patriotic "Canada First", and author of *Tecumseh: A Drama*. They had one son. He married for a second time in 1899 Mabel Lilias, daughter of Sir. Alexander T. Galt, one of the Fathers of Confederation, and brother of Elliot T. Galt who became a pioneer in railway and irrigation projects in southern Alberta. They had two daughters. He died in October 1949, at Victoria at the age of eighty-nine years.

Patrick Morgan Mahoney, *Liberal for Calgary South 1968-Present*

Born at Winnipeg in 1929, he was educated at Calgary and the University of Alberta (B.A. and LL.B. degree). A corporation executive, he has been active in promoting professional football. He was a president of the Canadian Football League and also president of the Stampede football club. He was first elected to the federal Parliament for Calgary South in the 1968 general election by defeating Ray Ballard, the incumbent Conservative member. His majority was under eight hundred in a three-way contest that saw close to 23000 votes cast. On January 28, 1972, Mahoney was appointed by Prime Minster Trudeau, Minister of State with special responsibility for continuing review of tax policy.

James Alexander Marshall, *Social Credit for Camrose 1935-1949*

Born in Lurgen Ireland in 1888, he was educated there, and at the Kildare Training College for teachers in Dublin. He came to Canada in 1912 to become a teacher in the Bashaw district of Alberta. He married in 1915 Edna Lawrence of Iowa, United States. His only daughter, Margaret Maureen married Randolph McKinnon, an Edmonton school teacher, who was a

Social Credit Minister of Education in Manning's administration in the 1960's. Marshall was the municipal secretary and entered federal politics in 1935 when he was elected for the Camrose constituency. He represented the riding in Ottawa for the next fourteen years. He was not a candidate in 1949. Religion: Anglican.

Donald Frank Mazankowski, *Progressive Conservative for Vegreville 1968-Present*

Born at Viking, Alberta in 1935, he is of Polish descent. Educated at Viking, he is a successful Vegreville businessman. He was a trustee on the Vegreville separate school board from 1963 to 1968. He entered federal politics in the 1968 general election. His majority was 10789 votes. Religion: Catholic.

Maitland Stewart McCarthy, *Conservative for Calgary 1904-1911*

Born at Orangeville, Ontario in 1872, he was the son of Judge McCarthy and his wife, Jennie Frances Stewart, both Irish. He was educated at Port Hope, Ontario, and Trinity University, Toronto (B.A. degree). he established his law practice in Calgary and entered politics in 1904 when he stood as the Conservative candidate for the Calgary seat in the Commons. He was successful and represented Calgary in Ottawa for the next seven years. In 1908, the provincial leadership of the Conservative party was offered him. McCarthy refused it on the ground that to resign his seat would compromise his honor, for his election had been protested and, until the case was decided, resignation would look like an admission of guilt. He was not a candidate in 1911. He was named a judge in 1914. He deid in May 1930, at Montreal. Religion: Anglican.

Dr. Wilbert MacIntyre, *Liberal for Strathcona 1905-1909*

Born at Rosedale, Ontario in 1867, he was of British descent. He was educated at Owen Sound Collegiate Institute and the University of Toronto where he obtained a Bachelor of Medicine degree. he came west as a young man and started to practice at Strathcona. He was a successful physician. Dr. MacIntyre because the president of the Strathcona Board of Trade in 1904. He entered federal politics as the Liberal candidate for Strathcona in the by-election caused when Peter Talbot was appointed to the Senate in 1905. He defeated his only opponent, Conservative Dr. Crang. He died while a sitting Member of Parliament in 1909, after being re-elected the year before. Religion: Presbyterian.

Archibald Hugh Mitchell, *Social Credit for Medicine Hat 1935-1945*

Born at Macleod, Alberta in 1903, he was the son of Archibald Mitchell who was of British descent. He was educated at Claresholm Agricultural College and the University of Alberta. Mitchell was a farmer in the Medicine at district. He entered federal politics in

1935 when he ran as a Social Credit candidate for Medicine Hat. In this election, he defeated incumbent Liberal Dr. Gershaw. However, five years later, Gershaw was able to recapture the riding. On his defeat in 1940, Mitchell retired from politics.

Harry Andrew Moore, *Progressive Conservative for Wetaskiwin 1962-Present*

Born at Wetaskiwin in 1914, he was educated at Wetaskiwin, Camrose normal school and the University of Alberta. He is a successful dairy farmer. First elected to the Commons in 1962, he has been re-elected in the general elections in 1963, 1965, and 1968. In 1972, he failed to be re-nominated as the Conservative candidate. Religion: United Church.

Carl Olof Nickel, *Progressive Conservative for Calgary South 1951-1957*

He was born at Winnipeg in 1914. His father's people came to America in 1842 from Ireland while his mother's family originally came from Sweden. Educated at Calgary's Mount Royal College, he started his own business in 1937 as publisher of Daily Oil Bulletin and weekly publication, Oil in Canada. Nickel entered federal politics in a buy-election caused by the death of Arthur Smith. He ran as a Progressive Conservative candidate for the Calgary South riding and won. He held the seat for six years before retiring from politics. He is an Anglican.

Terrence James Nugent, *Progressive Conservative for Edmonton Strathcona 1958-1968*

Born at Taber, Alberta in 1920, he was the son of Patrick Nugent and Bridget Duke, both Canadians of British descent. He was educated at Camrose, Edmonton, and the University of Alberta where he obtained a B.A. and an LL.B. degree. He served in the Canadian Air Force during the Second World War before he established his law practice in Edmonton. He was an unsuccessful Tory candidate in the 1957 federal election but won the Edmonton Strathcona riding in the 1958 election. He had a colorful career for ten years before being defeated by Liberal Dr. Hu Harris in the 1968b general election. Nugent then turned to civic politics and was elected an Edmonton alderman. He served for one term.

Frank Oliver, *Independent for Alberta 1896; Liberal for Alberta and the Edmonton 1900-1917; Minister of the Interior 1905-1911*

Born at Chinguacousy, Ontario in 1853, he was the son of Allan Bowsfield. His mother's maiden name was Oliver, which he adopted as his own. He worked on a number of newspapers in Ontario before moving to the Northwest Territories in the 1870s. In 1876, he began freighting by cart into Edmonton, which was only a village at the time. In 2880 Oliver founded Alberta's first newspaper, The Edmonton Bulletin, over which he retained control until 1923. He was always interested in politics and became a member of the North West Council in 1883. He was elected to the Legislative Assembly, which successes the Council with wider powers, 1888-1896. He was the Member of Parliament for some twenty years, commencing in 1896. On the resignation of Clifford Sifton in 1905, Oliver joined the Laurier cabinet as Minister of the interior and Superintendent of Indian Affairs. He remained the federal cabinet Minister for Alberta until the defeat of the western prairies. He was one of the few prominent western Liberals to support Laurier in the 19177 general election. He led General Griesbach in the civil vote, but failed to obtain a majority of the service votes cast. He then retired from active politics at the age of sixty-four. He was appointed a member of the Board of railway Commissioners in 1923 and served for five years. When Alberta was created a province in 1905, there was a strong possibility that Oliver would become the first Premier. However, he was more interested in obtaining a federal cabinet appointment, which he obtained that year. He died in March, 1933 at Ottawa.

Horace Andrew (Bud) Olson, *Social Credit for Medicine Hat 1957-1958; Liberal for Medicine Hat 1968-Present; Minister of Agriculture 1968-Present*

Born at Iddesleigh, Alberta in 1925, he is of Norwegian descent. His parents were born in North Dakota and came to Canada in 1912. He was educated at Iddesleigh and Medicine Hat. He is a farmer and merchant and has a large farm in the Rainy Hills district of Alberta. He entered federal politics as a Social Crediter and won the Medicine Hat riding in 1957. He was defeated by Ted Brunsden in the Diefenbaker landslide in March 1958. However, he captured the seat again for the Social Credit in 1962 and sat with Robert Thompson, the Social Credit National Leader until the spring of 1968 when he crossed the floor of the House to join the Liberals. He ran in the general election of that year as a Liberal and held the seat. He was named to the Trudeau cabinet in 1968 as the Minister of Agriculture. He is actively interested in Western Canadian history. Religion: Lutheran.

Steven Eugene Paproski, Progressive Conservative for Edmonton Centre 1968-Present

Born at Lvov, Poland in 1928, he is of Ukrainian descent. He was educated in Edmonton, University of North Dakota, University of Arizona and Banff School of Advanced management. He is a general sales manager. He was first elected to Parliament in 1968 for the urban constituency of Edmonton Centre in a four way contest. Former mayor William Hawrelak ran as an Independent Liberal candidate and thus split the Liberal vote. His brother, Dr. Ken Paproski, is the Progressive Conservative member for Edmonton Kingways in the Alberta Legislature (1972). He is a Roman Catholic.

Rene-Antoine Pelletier, *Social Credit for Peace River 1935-1940*

Born at St. Faustin, Quebec in 1908,, he was the son of Paul Z. Pelletier and Odila St. Jean, both French Canadians. He was a grand-nephew of the late Justice Pelletier of the Supreme Court of Quebec. Pelletier was educated at Montreal and Calgary, and worked as the station agent at Falher in the Peace River district of northern Alberta. He was an unsuccessful candidate in the 1935 provincial election. The same year he was the Social Credit candidate for the large Peace River riding and was successful in defeating the incumbent D.M. Kennedy. In 1940, he was in turn defeated by Liberal lawyer J.H. Sissons. He was a Roman Catholic.

Eric Joseph Poole, *Social Credit for Red Deer 1935-1940*

Born at Northwich, Cheshire, England in 1907, he was the son of Oswald James Poole and Helen Igo, both British. He was educated at Hennington Park, Northwich, before coming to Canada in 1909. However, he did not remain in this country for long but returned to the United Kingdom. He returned again to Canada in 1928 when he established Poole Construction, which is today one of the largest construction firms in western Canada. He entered federal politics in 1935 as a Social Credit candidate for Red Deer. He won the seat. Poole did not seek re-election five years later but retired permanently from politics. He is a Roman Catholic.

George Prudham, *Liberal for Edmonton West 1949-1957; Minister of Mines 1950-1957*

Born in Kilbride, Ontario in 1904, he is of British descent. Ancestors on his mother's side (her name was Anna Pickett) were United Empire Loyalist. He was educated at Waterdown, Ontario and Hamilton Technical School and became a wealthy building supply dealer, and was named president of the National House Builders Association of Canada. He was first elected to the Commons in 1949 and was named to the federal cabinet the next year. He did not have a distinguished political career, and retired from the federal arena in 1957. Religion: United Church.

Victor Quelch, *Social Credit for Acadia 1935-1958*

Born at Georgetown, British Guiana in 1891, he was the son of British parents. He was educated in the United Kingson at Fulneck College, leeds before coming to Canada in 1909. He joined the Canadian army five years later and saw active duty on the Western Front. He was awarded the MC in September 1918. On his return, he became a farmer. Quelch entered federal politics in 1935 when he captured the large central Alberta riding of Acadia from United Farmer incumbent Robert Gardiner. Quelch held the constituency until 1958 when he retied from politics. He is an Anglican.

Major Daniel Lee Redman, *Unionist for Calgary East 1917-1921*

Born at Oil City, Ontario in 1889, he was of English descent. He was educated at King's College, London, the Inns of Court, and the University of Manitoba where he obtained a law degree. He then settled in Calgary where he joined the law firm of Lougheed, Bennett and McLean. He became the director of several companies including Calgary Gas, Western Canada Natural Gas, and Alliance Power Company. He joined the Canadian expeditionary force in 1914, and saw active service on the Western Front. He was wounded at St. Julien in 1915. Redman entered politics in 1917 as a unionist candidate and served one term as a Member of Parliament for the city of Calgary. Redman was not a candidate in 1921.

Harris George Rogers, *Progressive Conservative for Red Deer, 1958-1962*

Born at Newton Robinson, Ontario in 1891, he is the son of Morrison Rogers and Elizabeth Campbell, both Canadians of British descent. He was educated at Cockstown and Bradford, Ontario. He was a farmer in the Red Deer district. He saw active military service in both the Great War and the Second World War. He was awarded the Military Cross for bravery while serving with a Calgary tank regiment. He was a Tory candidate in the 1957 federal election but was defeated. The next spring he carried the riding in the Diefenbaker landslide. He was defeated in 1962 by the then social Credit National Leader, Robert Thompson. Religion: United Church.

George Henry Ross, *Liberal for Calgary East 1940-1945*

Summoned to the Senate in 1948

(See: List of Senators)

Percy John Rowe, *Social Credit for Athabasca 1935-1940*

Born at Bowmanville, Ontario in 1893, he was the son of Roger Rowe and Laura Allin, both Canadians. He was educated at Port Hope, Ontario. He was trained as an accountant. When he came west as a young man he worked for nine years for the Standard Bank of Canada. He was the Mundare Branch manager of this bank from 1916 to 1919. Rowe was all his life interested in economics and banking and became a disciple of Major Douglas, the "father" of Social Credit. He was the secretary/treasurer of the town of Beverly from 1922 to 1933. Rowe entered federal politics in 1935 as the Social Credit candidate for Athabasca. He won the seat, defeating Conservative lawyer Davies. He was defeated in the 1940 general election by Liberal Joseph Dechene. Religion: United Church.

Stanley Stanford Schumacher, *Progressive Conservative for Palliser 1968-Present*

Born at Hanna, Alberta in 1933, he was educated at Drumheller, Calgary and at the University of British Columbia (B.Com., LL.B. degrees). He served as an officer with the RCAC before establishing his law practice at Drumheller. He entered federal politics for the first time in 1968 when he had a close to 8000 vote majority in the newly named Palliser constituency. He is an Anglican.

Frederick Davis Shaw, *Social Credit for Red Deer 1940-1958*

Born at Cardston in 1909, he was of United Empire Loyalist stcock. Educated at Cardston and Calgary normal school, he became a school teacher at Innisfail, Alberta. Shaw entered federal politics in 1940 when he became the Social Credit candidate for the Red Deer constituency. He was successful and sat in the House of Commons for the next eighteen years. He was defeated by Harris Rogers in the Diefenbaker landslide of March 1958. Religion: United Church.

Hugh Murray Shaw, *Unionist for Macleod 1917-1921*

Born at Kintore, Ontario in 1876, he was of British descent. He was educated at Kintore, High River and Calgary after coming west with his parents in 1901. He married in 1904 Annie Warren of Nanton. He became a successful farmer in the Nanton district and served on the municipal and school boards. He was elected in 1917 as unionist member for Macleod. He was defeated four years later by UFA George Coote. He died in April 1934, at Calgary. Religion: Methodist.

Joseph Tweed Shaw, *Labor for Calgary West 1921-1925*

Born at Port Arthur, Ontario in 1883, he was educated at Calgary and the University of Michigan where he obtained a Bachelor of Laws degree. He served in the Canadian Expeditionary Force on the Western Front during the Great War. On his return, besides practicing law, he entered federal politics and won one of the two urban ridings as a Labor candidate. He was defeated in his re-election bid four years later. He then turned to provincial politics and was elected as a Liberal for Bow Valley in the 1926 general election. Shaw served one term in the legislature as the leader of the opposition. He Arthur Lewis Sifton, Chief Justice of the Northwest Territories 1903-1905; Chief Justice of Alberta 1905-1910; Premier of Alberta 1910-1917; Minister of the Interior 1917-1921

Born at St. John's, near London, Ontario in 1858, he was the elder son of the Honorable John Wright Sifton. Clifford Sifton, Minister of the Interior in Laurier's cabinet, was his younger brother. He was educated in Winnipeg and at Victoria University, Coburg (B.A. 1880, M.A. 1888). He was called to the Bar of the Northwest Territories in 1883 and started to practice law in Brandon. He was named a Queen's Councillor in 1892, by which time he was practicing the legal profession in Calgary. Entering politics as a Liberal, he represented Banff in the territorial legislature 1899-1903, and served as Treasurer and Commissioner of Public Works in the Haultain administration. In 1903, he was named Chief Justice of the Supreme Court of the Northwest Territories and on the creation of the province of Alberta two years later he became its first Chief Justice. In 1910, he retired from the bench to become Alberta's second Premier. Besides being Premier, he was Provincial Treasurer, Minister of Public Works, and Minster of

Railways and Telephones. He represented Vermillion in the Legislature. In 1917, after leading his party successfully through a provincial election, he resigned his seat in order to enter federal politics. He had broken with Laurier over the conscription issue and ran successfully in the 1917 federal election as a Unionist candidate in Medicine Hat. He was named to Borden's national government as Minister of Customs. He was one of Canada's delegates to the peace conference at Versailles in 1919. In 1920, he was named the Secretary of State. He died in January 1921, at the age of sixty-two.

Professor L.G. Thomas in *The Liberal Party in Alberta (1959)* says that a fondness for the good things of life, cigars among them, did not redeem the lack of geniality that chilled his political allies and affronted his opponents. Sifton ruled the Liberal party in Alberta with an iron hand and it is difficult to avoid the conclusion that it was his vigorous personality that saved the party from the disaster that threatened it during the Alberta and Great Waterways episode. Yet, although he could hold the party together, he was not the man to heal the divisions which that crisis had only deepened, and once the "Czar" had abdicated, the Liberal party in Alberta began to disintegrate.

John Howard Sissons, *Liberal for Peace River, 1940-1945*

Born at Orillia, Ontario in 1892, he was of British descent. In the early 17th century, his ancestors, who were French Huguenots, left France and settled in

England. His mother was Jessie Livingstone, a cousin of the famous African explorer, Dr. David Livingstone. His father was the chief attendant at the Orillia Mental Asylum for thirty-five years. Sissons was educated at Queen's University where he obtained a Bachelor of Arts degree. He taught in small-town schools in Alberta for a couple of years while working his way through the university. He studied law in Edmonton and was called to the Alberta Bar in 1921. He practiced law for twenty-five years at Grande Prairie in the Peace River country. He was always active in politics and was named the Liberal candidate for the provincial riding of Clearwater in 1920. However, this northern Alberta constituency was abolished before the 1921 election, so he became a candidate without a riding. He was a member of the Grande Prairie School Board. In 1940 he entered federal politics as the Liberal candidate for Peace River. He won the seat by defeating the incumbent SoCred R.A. Pelletier. Five years later, he went down to defeat when Solon Low, the national Social Credit leader movement, won this vast northern Alberta riding. Prime Minister Mackenzie King the same year named Sisson a judge of the southern Alberta District Court. When the Territorial Court of the Northwest Territories was established in 1955, he became its first judge. He retired in 1966, and was awarded an honorary degree from The University of Lethbridge in 1969, shortly before his death. He wrote his autobiography, entitled Judge of the Far North in 1968.

William Skoreyko, *Progressive Conservative for Edmonton East 1958-Present*

Born at Edmonton in 1922, he is the son of Michael Skoreyko, who s of Ukrainian descent. He was educated at Edmonton and Senlac, Saskatchewan. He was a service station operator in 1958 when he was first elected to the federal house. He has held the urban Edmonton East riding for the past fourteen years. Religion: Greek Orthodox.

Clifford Smallwood, *Progressive Conservative for Battle River- Camrose 1958-1968*

Born at Irma, Alberta in 1915, he was the son of Robert Smallwood and Margaret McKay, both of British descent. He was educated at Irma and Edmonton. He is a successful farmer in the Irma district of Alberta. Smallwood was an unsuccessful Tory candidate in the 1957 general election. However, he took the Battle River-Camrose riding in the general election that next year and held it for the next ten years. He retired from federal politics in 1968. In 1971, he entered provincial politics and ran against Social Credit Agriculture Minister Henry Ruste. He was unsuccessful, even though Conservative Peter Lougheed was able to topple the thirty-six-year-old SoCred government. Religion: United Church.

Arthur Leroy Smith, *Progressive Conservative for Calgary West 1945-1951*

Born at Regina, Saskatchewan in 1886, he was the son of Jacob Watson Smith who was of British descent. He was educated at Regna and the University of Manitoba where he obtained a Bachelor of Arts degree. In 1912, he married Sara Isabel, daughter of Thomas Ryan of Winnipeg. They had two children, a daughter and a son, Arthur Ryan. (See: Arthur Ryan Smith, Progressive Conservative MP for Calgary South 1957-1963). Smith established his legal practice in Calgary. He first became active in politics in 1921 when he was an unsuccessful Conservative candidate in a federal election that saw the United Farmers of Alberta and their labor allies take every riding in the province. Smith ran again in 1945 and was elected in Calgary West. He was re-elected four years later, but resigned his seat in the Commons n November 1951. Carl Nickel held the seat for the Tories in the resulting by-election. He was an Anglican. He died December 17, 1951.

Arthur Ryan Smith, Progressive Conservative for Calgary South 1957-1963

Born at Calgary in 1919, he was son of Arthur Leroy Smith, a Calgary lawyer who sat in the Commons as a Progressive Conservative during the 1940s. He was educated at Shawnigan School, British Columbia. He joined the Royal Canadian Air Force during the Second World War and saw active service in Europe. He was awarded the Distinguished Flying Cross in 1944. Smith became an executive in the petroleum industry. He first became interested in civic politics, serving a three-year term on the Calgary city council. In 1955, he was one of the three Tories elected to the Legislature. Two years later, he resigned his seat in order to enter federal politics. He, with fellow Clagarian Douglas Harkness and Edmonton lawyer Marcel Lambert were the only Conservatives elected in 1957 that saw Diefenbaker form a minority government. He was re-elected in the 1958 federal election with one of the largest majorities in the whole of Canada. He had a 22, 443 vote majority over his nearest rival. He retired from politics in 1963. He sat in the Commons for six years before retiring from federal politics to return to industry at the age of forty-six. He is an Anglican.

James Alexander Smith, *Social Credit for Battle River-Camrose 1955-1958*

Born at Bawlf, Alberta in 1911, he was the son of Thomas E. Smith, who was of British descent. He was educated at Czar, Edmonton, the University of Alberta and Montana State University at Missoula. Smith taught in several schools in Alberta from 1932-1955, including Czar, Paradise Valley and Kitscoty. He was the president of the Alberta Teacher's Association (ATA) for one term. Smith entered federal politics as a Social Crediter in 1955 when he ran in the by-election in Battle River-Camrose caused by the death of the sitting Member SoCred Robert Fair. He was successful and was re-elected two years later but was unable to hold the seat against the Diefenbaker ride in 1958. Religion: United Church.

Alfred Speakman, *UFA for Red Deer 1921-1935*

Born at Dundee, Scotland in 1880, he was the son of James Speakman and Mary Hanna Farrar. The Speakmans came to Canada when Alfred was a child in 1891. He was a successful farmer in the Red Deer district for many years and was active in the UFA organization. He entered federal politics as a candidate in the 1921 general election and sat for a total of fourteen years in Parliament. He was defeated in the Social Credit sweep of 1935. Speakman came out of retirement to run as Independent in the 1940provincial election. He won the provincial constituency of Red Deer and died while still an MLA in November 1943, at Edmonton. Religion: United Church.

James Stanley Speakman, *Progressive Conservative for Wotaskiwin 1958-1962*

Born at Penhold, Alberta in 1906, he was the son of James Farrar Speakman and Eva Richards, both of British descent. He was a relation of Alfred Speakman. He was educated at Victoria High School, Edmonton, and became a general accountant in Wetaskiwin. Speakman served as an office in the Canadian Army from 1943 to 1957. He was an unsuccessful candidate in the June 1957 election, but was victorious in March 1958, when the province went completely Conservative. He died while still an MP in April 1962. Religion: United Church.

Henry Elvis Spencer, *UFA for Battle River 1921-1935*

Born near Alcester, England in 1882, he worked in a bank prior to going to France in 1906 where he learnt the publishing business. He came to Canada in 1908 where he homesteaded in the Edgerton district. He became a successful farmer and was active in the UFA, being the director for Battle River from 1917 to 1921. Spencer represented the UFA interests in the Commons for fourteen years commencing in 1921. Religion: Unitarian.

Dr. George Douglas Stanley, *Conservative for Calgary East 1930-1935*

Born at Exeter, Ontario in 1876, he was the son of Thomas Stanley and Hannah Westman, both Canadians. His father was a former mayor of St. Mary's, Ontario. He was educated at St. Mary's Collegiate and the University of Toronto where he obtained a degree in medicine. After graduation, Stanley came west to Calgary where he became a prominent physician and stalwart prohibitionist. He became interested in provincial politics and ran unsuccessfully as a Conservative in the 1909 general election. He was victorious on his second attempt four years later when he was elected for the High River constituency. He was re-elected in 1917 and was the most fervent Conservative crusader for temperance in the Legislature, claiming that judges were drunk in hotel corridors at night and next morning sat in judgment on those on trial for breaches of the Liquor

Act. He retired from provincial politics in 1921 after becoming the president of the Alberta College of Physicians and Surgeons. He entered federal politics successfully in 1930 when he was elected the Conservative Member for the urban riding of Calgary East with a large 5342 vote majority. For years, Dr. Stanley was next to R.B. Bennett as one of the most important Conservatives in the province. He died in February 1954. Religion: United Church.

Peter Stefura, *Social Credit for Vegreville 1957-1958*

Born at Chipman, Alberta in 1923, he was the son of William Stefura and Helen Diduck, both Ukrainians. He was educated at Hilliard, Chipman and at the Edmonton normal school. He was a farmer in the Chipman district and operated the Chipman Creamery. Stefura was a councillor and reeve of the municipal district of Lamont. He entered federal politics as a Social Crediter in 1957 when he was elected in the Vegreville riding. He was defeated in the next federal election held nine months later by Conservative Frank Fane. Religion: Ukrainian Greek Orthodox.

Charles Stewart, *Premier of Alberta 1917-1921; Liberal for Argenteuil (Quebec) 1922-1925; Liberal for Edmonton West 1925-1935; Minister of the Interior and of Mines 1921-1925; Minister of the Interior 1926-1930*

Born at Strabane, Ontario in 1868, he was of British descent. Educated at Stabane, he came to the

Northwest Territories at the turn of the century and homesteaded in the Killam district of Alberta. He became a successful farmer. Elected by acclamation to the Legislature in 1909 as the Liberal Member for Sedgewick, he held the central Alberta riding uintil he resigned in order to enter federal politics in 1922. Stewart rose rapidly in the government of Premier Sifton, serving successively as Minister of Municipal Affairs and Minister of Public Works. When Sifton resigned to become a member of Robert Borden's Union cabinet in 1917, Stewart was chosen to become the third Premier of Alberta. He also held the post of Minister of Railways and Telephones. Despite his personal popularity, his government was defeated by the United Farmers of Alberta in the 1921 general election. He first resigned the premiership and then his seat in the Legislature.

As a result of the 1921 election, not a single Liberal was elected in Alberta. Prime Minister Mackenzie King appointed Stewart to his cabinet and found him a safe set in Quebec to run in order to get him into the federal House. He was returned for Edmonton West in the 1925 election and retained the seat until 1935. He retired from active politics that year at the age of sixty-seven. The next year, he was appointed Canadian chairman of the International Joint Commission and held this office until his death ten years later. He died in December 1946, at Ottawa. He was an Anglican.

John Smith Stewart, *MLA for Lethbridge 1911-1925; Conservative for Lethbridge 1930-1935*

Born at Brampton, Ontario in 1878, he was the son of John Stewart and Mary Armstrong, both Canadians. He was educated at the University of Toronto where he obtained a dental degree in 1903. Prior to that, he had seen active service in the Boer War as a private in Strathcona's Horse. For more than half a century he was one of the leading dentists in Lethbridge. He also had a distinguished military career. During the Great War, he was awarded the DSO and the Croix de Guerre. He rose to the rank of general. Stewart was first elected to the Alberta Legislature in 1911 as a Conservative. He sat in the provincial House for fourteen years. In 1921, he refused to become the Speaker. In 1925, he failed in his first attempt to get elected to the Commons. However, five years later, he was successful and represented Lethbridge in Ottawa for five years. He died in 1970. Religion: United Church.

Allen Sulatycky, *Liberal for Rocky Mountain 1968-Present*

Born at Hafford, Saskatchewan in 1938, he is of Ukrainian descent. He was educated at Hafford and the University of Saskatchewan (B.A. and LL.B. degrees. After graduation, he established his law practice at Whitecourt, Alberta. He entered federal politics in 1967 when he stood as the Liberal candidate in the Jasper-Edson by-election caused when Dr. Hugh Horner resigned his seat in Parliament to enter provincial politics. He was defeated by Conservative Doug Caston. He ran the next year in the general election in newly-created constituency of Rocky Mountain, which includes the National Parks of Waterton, Banff and Jasper. This was a six-way contest. The Conservative vote was split by Caston running as an Independent Conservative. Religion: Greek Orthodox.

Peter Talbot, *Liberal for Strathcona 1904-1906*

Summoned to the Senate in 1906

(See: List of Senators)

Ray Thomas, *Social Credit for Wetaskiwin 1949-1958*

Born at Mirror, Alberta in 1917, he was the son of George Melvin Thomas (Welsh) and Zella Ray, his American wife. Educated at Mirror and Mount Royal College, Calgary, he served five years with the Royal Canadian Navy during the Second World War. He returned to become a merchant in Wetaskiwin. Thomas entered federal politics in 1969 when he was the Social Credit candidate for the central Alberta riding of Wetaskiwin. He was elected by a narrow 683 vote majority. He represented the constituency in the Commons for the next nine years before being defeated by Conservative James Speakman in 1958. Religion: United Church.

Robert Norman Thompson, *Social Credit for Red deer 1962-1968; National Social Credit Leader 1961-*

1968; Progressive Conservative for Red Deer 1968-Present

Born at Duluth, Minnesota in 1914, he was the son of Theodore Thompson and Hannah Olufson, both Canadians. He was educated at Garbutt's Business College, Calgary normal school, Palmer College, Bob Jones University and the University of British Columbia. He was active in 1935 in Manitoba on behalf of the Social Credit movement. At the outbreak of the Second World War, Thompson joined the Canadian Air Force and saw active service in the Middle East. In 1945, he was the director of the Imperial Ethiopian Air Force training program. He later became the Minister of Education for Ethiopia and worked in that African nation in the field of education for fifteen years before returning to Canada in 1960. On his return he was elected president of the Social Credit Association of Canada. It was while he was the SoCred national leader that the party elected thirty members to the House of commons, four from western Canada and twenty-six from Quebec. He, himself, was elected in the central Alberta riding of Red Deer. In 1968, he changed his political affiliations and joined the Conservatives. He was re-elected that year as a Tory. He is an expert on African affairs, and refers to himself as an educator. In 1972, he announced he was moving to British Columbia and would not seek re-election. Religion: Protestant.

Syd Thompson, *Social Credit MP for Edmonton-Strathcona 1957-1958*

Born in Athabasca in 1920, he was educated at Rabbit Hill, Alberta. After having a go at banking, he joined the RCAF and saw active service during the Second World War. On his return from the war, he became the manager of a large food market in South Edmonton. He entered federal politics in 1957 when he was a successful Social Credit candidate. In the next general election nine months later, he was defeated by Conservative Terry Nugent.

Stanley G. Tobin, *Liberal for Wetaskiwin 1925-1926*

Born at Bridgewater, Nova Scotia in 1871, he was of British descent. He was educated at Bridgewater Academy before going to the Pictou Academy. He trained as a school teacher and taught for several years in Alberta before he entered business. He became interested in provincial politics in 1913 when he was elected the Liberal member of the Legislature for Leduc. He was able to hold his seat when the United Farmers swept to power in 1921. In 1925, he resigned his seat in the Legislature to run federally for the Wetaskiwin riding. He was successful, but was defeated by William Irvine in the general election of 1926.

Thomas Mitchell March Tweedie, *Conservative-Unionist for Calgary West 1917-1921*

Born at River John, Nova Scotia in 1871, he was of British descent. His father was a Methodist minister. He was educated at Pictou Academy, Mount Allison University, and Harvard University (B.A. and LL.B.

degrees). He established his law practice in Calgary at the turn of the century. Tweedie first entered provincial politics in 1911, in a by-election held to fill the vacancy caused by the resignation of R.B. Bennett when he ran in the federal election that yaer. He remained in the Legislature until 1917 when he, too, ran federally as a Conservative-Unionist candidate. Tweedie had the largest majority in the province of some 6971 votes. He served one term in Ottawa and was not a candidate in 1921. He was appointed a judge the same year by Prime Minister Meighan. In 1944, he was named Chief Justice of the Trial Division of the Supreme Court of Alberta. He died in October 1944, at Lethbridge. Religion: Methodist.

David E. Warnock, *Liberal for Macleod 1911-1917*

Born at Hamilton, Lanarkshire, Scotland in 1865, he was educated at Hamilton Grammar School and Glasgow Veterinary College (degree MRCVS) before coming to Canada. A veterinary surgeon and farmer, he was the Dominion veterinary inspector from 1904 to 1909. He entered provincial politics in 1909, when he was the successful liberal candidate in the Pincer Creek riding. He resigned his seat in the Legislature two years later in order to enter federal politics, and run in the Macleod constituency, he won the election, and did not seek a second term in the next federal election six years later. While he was in the Legislature, Warnock was one of the leading "insurgent Liberals" against Alberta and Great

Waterways Railway contracts in the debate that resulted in Premier Rutherford quitting. Warnock moved to British Columbia in 1919 when he became the Deputy Minister of Agriculture until 1928. He died by drowning in August 1932 in the Straits of Georgia. Religion: Presbyterian.

Daniel Webster Warner, *UFA for Strathcona 1921-1925*

Born at Richland, Iowa, United States in 1857, he was the son of Gideon Webster and Matilda, his wife, who were both Americans. He was educated at public schools in Iowa and Nebraska before he came north into Canada at the turn of the century. Warner became a farmer and stockraiser in the district south of Edmonton. He became the director of the Edmonton city dairy and the Edmonton Exhibition Company. He was active for many years in the United Farmers movement. In 1917, he received the Liberal nomination to contest the Battle River riding. He as defeated by Conservative W.J. Blair. Four years later, he ran in the Strathcona riding as the official United Farmers of Alberta candidate and was elected. He sat in the federal House only for one term. He died in May 1933 at Edmonton. Religion: Methodist.

John William Welborn, *Liberal for Jasper-Edson 1949-1953*

Born at Edmonton in 1900, he as the G.J. Welborn, a Canadian. He was educated at Winterburn, Edmonton and at the Vermillion Agricultural College. In 1927, he married Muriel, daughter of W.G. Talbot of Edmonton, Welborn was an unsuccessful farmer. He entered federal politics in 1945 when he was an unsuccessful Liberal candidate. Four years later, he was elected to the Commons on his second attempt for the large rural riding of Jasper-Edson. He was defeated in the 1953 general election when SoCred Yuill won the seat. Religion: United Church.

William Henry White, *Liberal for Victoria 1908-1921*

Born at View City, Ontario in 1865, he was educated at Ottawa. He came west as a young man in 1881 to join the North West Mounted Police. He served six years with the force before homesteading in the Fort Saskatchewan district. He entered federal politics in 1908 as a Liberal candidate. He was successful and was re-elected in 1911 and 1917. In the later election, White was one of the two Laurier Liberals to be elected in Alberta – Buchanan of Lethbridge was the other. He died in June 1930 at Fort Saskatchewan. He was an Anglican.

Eldon Woolliams, *Progressive Conservative for Bow River 1958-1968; Progressive Conservative for Calgary North 1968-Present*

Born at Rosetown, Saskatchewan in 1916, he is the son of Frank Woolliams who was of British descent. He was educated at rural schools in Saskatchewan and at the University of Saskatchewan where he obtained a degree in law. He was called to the Saskatchewan Bar in 1944 and to the Alberta Bar eight years later. He was named a Queen's Councillor in 1964. He was active in politics in his native province before he came to Alberta in the earl7 1950s. his first attempt to obtain a seat in the Commons in 1957 was unsuccessful. However, in the federal election called by Prime Minister Diefenbaker nine months later, he won the Bow River for the Tories by defeating incumbent Social Crediter Johnston. He has been re-elected in the 1962, 1963, 1965 and 1968 federal elections, the last for the urban riding of Calgary north. He is an Anglican.

William Duncan McKay Wylie, *Social Credit for Medicine Hat 1945-1957*

Born at Kirriemuir, Forfarshire, Scotland in 1900, he came to Canada as a boy in 1913 and was educated in Scotland and at Lougheed, Alberta. He worked for years as a provincial civil servant, first for the Department of Agriculture and then for the Department of Municipal Affairs as an inspector. Wylie entered federal politics in 1945 when he was the Social Credit candidate for Medicine Hat. Wylie defeated the incumbent Liberal Dr. Fred Gershaw and held the constituency until he retired in 1957. Religion: United Church.

Paul Yewchuk, *Progressive Conservative for Athabasca 1968-Present*

Born in 1937 in Lac La Biche, Alberta, he son of John Yewchuk, who came to Canada as a child. Educated at Lac La Biche and the University of Alberta, he was granted a medical degree in 1962. He then established his practice in Lac La Biche. Dr. Yewchuk entered federal politics in 1968 when he ran as the Conservative candidate in the large northern Alberta riding of Athabasca. He won the three-way struggle with a twelve-hundred vote majority. In so doing, he defeated former provincial Liberal leader and mayor of Athabasca, Mike Maccagno. In 1971 Dr. Yewchuk, with the help of young Irish doctor, Desmond Dwyer, set up his own northern flying doctor service. This service, using one airplane, now operates out of Fort McMurray.

Charles Yuill, *Social Credit for Jasper-Edson 1953-1958*

Born at Calabogie, Ontario in 1889, he was the son of John Yuill and Laurel Bailey. He was educated at Calabogie and Edmonton before becoming a merchant in the town of Barrhead, Alberta.

Yuill was elcted the mayor of Barrhead for seven terms before he entered federal politics in 1953 as the Social Credit candidate for Jasper-Edson. He was successful on his first attempt to enter the Commons by defeating Liberal incumbent John Welbourn. He was re-elected in 1957, but went down to defeat at the hands of Conservative Dr. Hugh Horner in the 1958 Diefenbaker sweep of the province. He was unsuccessful in his attempt to unseat Horner in the 1962 federal election.

Chapter Four

Federal and Provincial Administrations

Since the province of Alberta was created in 1905, the political party in power in Edmonton has been different and in conflict with the federal administration. The only exception was the first six years of the province's existence when the Liberals were in office both in Edmonton and in Ottawa. But in 1911, Sir Wilfrid Laurier was defeated by the Conservatives led by Robert Borden. It was in this election that Calgary lawyer and Member of the Legislature R.B. Bennett was first elected to the federal House. Twenty years later he became the Prime Minister of Canada.

The Liberals held the reins of power in Alberta until 1921 when the United Farmers of Alberta swept them out of office. Henry Wise Wood, originally an American from Missouri who had bought a farm in Alberta in 1905, was the UFA president. However, he refused to become the Premier, even though he was referred to as the "uncrowned King of Alberta". The United Farmers were in power for the next fourteen years, and were only defeated after a series of scandals involving cabinet ministers had discredited the government in the eyes of the voting public.

The Social Credit movement led by schoolteacher and radio evangelist William Aberhart was victorious in the depression election of 1935. He was the Premier, despite a backbencher revolt, until his death eight years later. His assistant in the Calgary

Prophetic Bible Institute, Ernest Manning, then became Premier. He led his party to seven consecutive victories at the polls in the next twenty-five years. He ran very much a one-man government holding at one time or another several of the most important portfolios. He retired undefeated in December 1968. It was due in no small part tp tis Baptist minster's personality that the Progressive Conservatives failed to capitalize provincially on their federal sweep of the province in 1958. Harry Strom, Manning's successor, did not have the charisma of the former Premier and was defeated in an upset election by the Progressive Conservatives in August 1971. Thus, after being outside the main stream of Canadian political life for fifty years, Alberta is being governed by of the two main political parties. If Robert Stanfield's Progressive Conservative can defeat the Liberals in the forthcoming federal election set for the fall of 1972, the same political party will be in power both in Edmonton and Ottawa.

Premiers of Alberta

Premier	Term of Office	Governing Party
A.C. Rutherford	1905-1910	Liberal
Arthur Sifton	1910-1917	Liberal

Charles Stewart	1917-1921	Liberal
Herbert Greenfield	1921-1925	United Farmers of Alberta
John Brownlee	1925-1934	United Farmers of Alberta
Richard Reid	1934-1935	United Farmers of Alberta
William Aberhart	1935-1943	Social Credit
Ernest C. Manning	1943-1969	Social Credit
Harry Strom	1969-1971	Social Credit
Peter Lougheed	1971-Present	Progressive Conservative

Premiers: Age When Named Premier

30-39	1
40-47	3
50-59	6

Occupations of Premiers

Law	4
Farming	4
Ministry	2
Education	1

Federal and Provincial Administration

1905-1972

Date	Federal Government	Provincial Government	Alberta's Representative in the Federal Government
1905	Liberal (Laurier)	Liberal (Rutherford)	Oliver
1905	Liberal (Laurier)	Liberal (Rutherford)	Oliver
1911	Conservative (Borden)	Liberal (Sifton)	Lougheed
1917	Unionists (Borden)	Liberal (Stewart_	Sifton
1920	Unionist (Meighen)	Liberal (Stewart)	Bennett
1921	Liberal (Mackenzie-King)	United Farmers (Greenfield)	---
1925	Conservative (Meighen)	United Farmers (Greenfield)	Bennett
1926	Liberal (Mackenzie-King)	United Farmers (Brownlee)	---
1930	Conservative (Bennett)	United Farmers	Bennett

Year			
		(Brownlee)	
1934	Conservative (Bennett)	United Farmers (Reid)	Bennett
1935	Liberal (Mackenzie-King)	Social Credit (Aberhart)	MacKinnon
1943	Liberal (Mackenzie-King)	Social Credit (Manning)	MacKinnon
1949	Liberal (St. Laurent)	Social Credit (Manning)	Prudham
1957	Progressive Conservative (Diefenbaker)	Social Credit (Manning)	Harkness
1963	Progressive Conservative (Diefenbaker)	Social Credit (Manning)	Lambert
1963	Liberal (Pearson)	Social Credit (Manning)	Hays
1968	Liberal (Trudeau)	Social Credit (Manning)	Olson
1969	Liberal (Trudeau)	Social Credit (Strom)	Olson
1971	Liberal (Trudeau)	Progressive Conservative (Lougheed)	Olson
1972	Liberal (Trudeau)	Progressive Conservative (Lougheed)	Olson and Mahoney

An Alphabetical List of the Premiers of Alberta with a Brief Biographical Sketch

William Aberhart, Seventh Premier of Alberta
1935-1943

Born December 30, 1878, on a farm near Seaforth, Ontario, he was the son of William Aberhart, a German immigrant, and Lousia Pepper. Educated at Seaforth and Chatham, young Aberhart then attended the normal school in Hamilton, becoming a teacher. He c continued his studies by summer school and by taking correspondence courses, until he obtained a Bachelor of Arts degree from Queen's University in 1906. He came west to Calgary four years later as a teacher. By 1915, he was the principal of Crescent Heights High School, a position he held for the next twenty years.

Besides carrying out his duties as a school teacher and administrator, Aberhart gave Bible classes on Sundays. The popularity of these classes led to the formation of the Calgary Prophetic Bible Institute of which he became Dean. The Institute's radio broadcasts became famous as "The Back to the Bible Hour" and on a very wide audience across the Canadian prairies. His religious ministry was primarily a radio ministry and such a medium "provides little for the records of the work done."

In the early 1930s he first encountered the Social Credit theories of Major C.H. Douglas. Profoundly impressed, Aberhart introduced Social Credit ideas into his religious radio broadcasts. He believed that they contained the answers for the economic ills that the depression had brought in its wake. He sought in vain to persuade the political parties existing in Alberta to incorporate monetary reforms into their platforms. When this failed, he organized a political movement based on the hundreds of study groups across the province. The Social Credit Movement ran a full slate of candidates, all handpicked by Aberhart. In the 1935 provincial election, fifty-six of the sixty-three seats were won by his followers. He accepted the premiership and got into the legislature when the Social Credit member for Okotoks-High river resigned, he was fifty-seven years of age when named Premier.

Once in office he found he had no ultimate solution to the problem of economics and government. He was blocked by the courts in his efforts to introduce a Social Credit program. After this rejection, Aberhart settled down to give Albertans good government. He was also able to withstand a backbenchers revolt.

His bid in Saskatchewan failed and thereafter, he turned his attention to handling Albertan affairs. He radically changed the educational system, introducing larger administrative units. His administration was re-elected with a reduced majority in 1940.

Claiming divine sanction for his party platform, Aberhart put a religious imprint on politics and the province for the next 36 years. His nickname was "bible Bill". A master showman, he dramatized each event and at times he seemed to equate his well publicized intent to pay the dividend ($25 to every

Albertan) with the accomplished fact. Although of his sincerity there was never any doubt, his mind seemed to be made up of compartments and he was undisturbed by the contradictions between his profession and practice.

William Aberhart aimed high in each field he entered. Reveling in organization, he won conspicuous success first as a teacher, then as a preacher, and finally as a politician. But fundamentally, in all his relations, he was school master. He spent most of his life in a classroom, and it was easy matter for him to become a political evangelist and treat the province as if it were one big classroom. His authoritarian manner and didactic dogmatism alienated many who were not blind to his human frailties, but by the same token, his drive and determination were an asset, enforcing through reforms that others had hesitated to carry out. Aberhart capitalized on the discontent of the Great Depression to fashion a religious and political crusade that he hoped would restore prosperity to the Prairies. He died while still the Premier in Vancouver, May 23rd 1943.

John Edward Brownlee, *Fifth Premier of Alberta 1925-1934*

Born August 27th in 1884, at Fort Ryerse, Ontario, he was the son of William James Brownlee and Christine Shaw, and was a member of the oldest families in the country. His paternal grandfather, Edward James Brownlee, was a native of the north of Ireland, and in early manhood, he came with his wife to Canada. Young Brownlee was educated in the public schools in Sarnia. He then spent three and a half years as a teacher at Bradshaw before he enrolled in the University of Toronto in 1904. He graduated with a Bachelor of Arts degree in 1908. After a year of traveling in the Prairie Provinces, he decided to settle in Calgary where he articled as a student in the law firm of Lougheed and Bennett. In 1912 he was admitted to the Alberta Bar. Some five years later, he became the legal advisor for the United Grain Growers of Winnipeg and the United Farmers of Alberta. After Henry Wisewood, Brownlee was the most influential person in the UFA movement. It was only because he was a lawyer that he was not named a Premier in 1921 when Wood refused the post. Nevertheless, even though he was not a Member of the Legislature, he was named the Attorney General in Greenfield's administration. He entered the Legislature when he was elected by acclamation in a by-election in Ponoka.

In 1923, he successful opposed radical financial resolutions that seemed to him to threaten provincial credit. Brownlee was Wood's choice for the premiership; he succeeded to that office in November 1925, when Greenfield resigned. During his administration the provincially-owned and operated Alberta and Great Waterways Railway and the Edmonton, Dunvegan and British Columbia Railway were sold to the Canadian National Railway. Control of Alberta's resources was transferred to the province by the federal government. Brownlee played an important part in these negotiations that ended a controversy which had existed since 1905. Brownlee, an imposing athletic figure, more than six feet tall, managed to make an indelible mark on the future of Alberta.

Brownlee's political career ended in a widely-publicized scandal in 1934, when he was sued for the seduction of an eighteen year old girl. The write had been issued through the Supreme Court channels and claimed unstated damages and costs. The suit had been entered by Allen C. MacMillan, father of the girl, Vivian MacMillan, and the girl herself who was employed as a stenographer at the Government Buildings. The civil action, in which the stated sum of $20000 was claimed from Brownlee, was heard in the latter part of June. It was concluded on July 1, the jury of six finding in favor of the plaintiff and awarding $10000 to Miss MacMillan and $5000 to her father. On June 30, the day before the conclusion of the case, an $8000 counter-claim of Premier Brownlee against Vivian MacMillan and John Coldwell, third year student at the University of Alberta, who had proposed marriage to Miss MacMillan, charging them with conspiracy to obtain money, had been dismissed by the judge. On July 4, Mr. W.C. Ives, who presided, rendered his judgment, dismissing the action with costs, which overruled the jury's verdict. Under the judgment the MacMillans were required to pay the legal costs of Brownlee as well as their own. An appeal was launched. The case was finally carried to the Judicial Committee of the Privy Council which, in 1940, sustained the original award.

Immediately after the jury's verdict, Premier Brownlee rendered his resignation to the Lieutenant-Governor. He, however, retained his seat in the Legislature, but was defeated by Mrs. Edith Rogers in the general election a year later. He then returned to his law practice. Brownlee later became general manager of the United Grain Growers, a farmer's co-operative. He retired in 1958. He died at the age of seventy-six in July 1961. Religion: Methodist.

Herbert Greenfield, *Fourth Premier of Alberta 1921-1925*

Born in 1865 at Winchester, England, he was the son of John Greenfield. He was educated at the Wesleyan School, Dalston, England for a short time. One of a large family, he halted his educated to go to work for a grain shopping firm in London and carried on studies of economics and trade on his own time. In 1892, he came to Canada and worked on an Ontario farm for the wage of $15 a month. He finally homesteaded in the Westlock district, north of Edmonton in 1906. He was forty-one years of age at the time. A participant in cooperatives in the United Kingdom and a successful farmer in Alberta, Greenfield was an active member and later became the vice-president of the United Farmers of Alberta. Following the victory of the UFA in the provincial election of 1921, he was chosen Premier only after Henry Wise Wood had declined and John Brownlee had been passed over because he was a lawyer. He was a compromise candidate, and proved not to be an unqualified success as provincial leader. He showed a lack of attention to public affairs which involved the government in considerable criticism and caused the Liberal opposition to assert that the people had lost faith in the administrative ability of the government. Distrust of Greenfield's leadership increased when he sponsored a resolution in favour of greater immigration. This was diametrically opposed to a resolution on the same subject adopted by the UFA convention. In November 1925, the long-expected resignation of Greenfield was announced and the elevation of Attorney General Brownlee to the premiership.

In 1927, he was named Agent General for Alberta in London, a post he held for four years. On his return to Alberta, Greenfield was associated with the petroleum industry. He was President and Managing Director of Calmont Oil of Calgary at the time of his death, which occurred in August 1949.

E. Peter Lougheed, Tenth Premier of Alberta 1971-Present

Born July 26, 1928, he was the son of Edgar Lougheed and Edna Bauld. His grandfather, Sir James Lougheed, was the Conservative leader in the Senate for many years and his grandmother was a member of the Hardisty family who were factors of the Hudson's Bay Company in Edmonton for years in the mid-19th century. He also related to Donald Smith who became Lord Strathcona. Young Lougheed was educated at Earl Grey and Calgary Central High School before he entered the University of Alberta. While working for a law degree, he as president of the students' union and a football player. After graduation, Lougheed went on to Harvard where he obtained a Masters degree in Business Administration. He put in two summers at army camps with the Canadian Officers' Training Corps. He also had other summer jobs ranging from driving a tourist bus at Banff to labouring for a construction firm. On his return to Calgary from the United States, he went to work for Mannix Construction, a large construction firm, as an executive. In a few years, he worked his way up to vice-president. Later, Lougheed resigned to go into law partnership. The law firm gave him to step into provincial politics. In February 1965, he was chosen as the provincial Progressive Conservative leader. Two years later, he was successful in his first bid to obtain a seat in the Legislature. Five other Conservatives were also elected. One was former MP Dr. Hugh Horner, who was the most experienced parliamentarian in the group. The Conservatives obtained twenty-six percent of the popular vote but, more important, Lougheed, in the following years, persuaded Albertans that his party was an acceptable alternative to the aging Social Credit administration that had been in power since the depression days of the 1930s.

The political climate in Alberta changed after Ernest Manning retired in December 1968. He has since been named to the Senate by Prime Minister Trudeau. The Progressive Conservatives won the resulting by-election and increased their strength in the House to ten by the time Premier Harry Strom called the provincial election in August 1971. Lougheed led his party to an upset victory. A total of 49 Conservatives were elected, compared to only 25 Social Crediters and one Socialist. The forty-three-year old Calgary lawyer-businessman was sworn in an Alberta's tenth Premier on September 10, 1971.

In 1952, he married Jeanne Estelle, daughter of Lawrence Rogers of Edmonton. They have four children. He is an Anglican.

Peter Lougheed is one of the few young Progressive Conservatives whose political star appears to be rising. In a few years time, he might listen to the siren song of federal politics – who at this time can tell. However, it is worth noting that no Canadian has become Prime Minister by way of premiership of one of the provinces.

Ernest Charles Manning, *Eighth Premier of Alberta 1943-1969*

(See: List of Senators)

Richard Gavin Reid, *Sixth Premier of Alberta 1934-1935*

Born January 17, 1879 in Glasgow, Scotland, he was the son of George Reid and Margaret Ogston. Educated in Glasgo, young Reid served in the

Medical Corps during the South African War. He left his native land in 1903 at the age of twenty-four years, and first settled at Killarney, Manitoba. Six months later, he went to the lumber camps of New Ontario, where he was employed for almost a year. He then moved to Edmonton. Later, he homesteaded in Saskatchewan but soon afterward, the boundary line was changed and his claim was then included within the confines of Alberta, where he was to reside for the rest of his life. He became a successful farmer in the Vermillion district. His worth and ability were soon recognized when he was elected first a member of the Council of Buffalo Coulee, and then acted as reeve of the municipality during a two-year period. On the organization of the Mannville Municipal Hospital District in 1918, Reid was made a member of its Board – this was the first Municipal Hospital District to be organized in the province. In the 1921 provincial election, Richard Reid was elected to represent Vermillion in the Legislature. He was appointed Minister of Health and Municipal Affairs in the Greenfield UFA government. Two years later, he was named the Provincial Treasurer. When John Brownlee became Premier in 1925, Reid was re-appointed to the cabinet as Provincial Treasurer and Minister of Municipal Affairs. When a scandal caused Brownlee to resign in July 1934, Reid was selected by the UFA members of the Legislature to be the Premier. He was also the Provincial Secretary. He went down to personal defeat as did all members of his party in 1935 when Social Credit won a sweeping victory.

In 1919, he married Marion Stuart of Mannville, Alberta; they had three sons and one daughter. Reid was highly thought of when he became Alberta's sixth Premier. *The Financial Post* at the time stated that "He is too thorough in his thinking to be an extremist; too deliberate to be a radical; too human to be a reactionary." Religion: Presbyterian.

Alexander Cameron Rutherford, *First Premier of Alberta 1905-1910*

Born February 2, 1857 at Osgoode, Carleton County, Ontario, he was the son of James Rutherford and Elizabeth Cameron, both natives of Aberfeldy, Perthshire, Scotland. He received his early education at Metcalfe and Woodstock before entering McGill University. After obtaining degrees in arts and law, he articled with R.W. Scott, a former Secretary of State in Ottawa. Rutherford practiced law in the federal capital for ten years before he came to Alberta in 1895. He established himself in Strathcona, then known as Edmonton South. Here he practiced law independently until 1900, when the firm, Rutherford and Jamieson, was formed.

Rutherford was Solicitor and Treasurer of Strathcona from 1899 to 1905, and was Secretary of the School Board from 1896 to 1905. He entered politics in 1902 and was elected a Member of the Legislature in support of the Haultain government of the Northwest Territories, from the Strathcona constituency, which at that time extended as far east as Saskatchewan. In his first session he was chosen Deputy Speaker of the House, which position he held until the formation of the new provinces. In august 1905, a Liberal convention was held in Calgary, at which Rutherford was unanimously selected the president of the party in Alberta. It was tacitly understood that whoever was chosen should be the first Premier of the province. Frank Oliver and Peter Talbot expressed no desire for the position.

On September 1, 1905, the Province of Alberta was inaugurated by Earl Grey and Rutherford was called on by Lieutenant-Governor Bulyea to form an administration. He served as Premier, Minister of Education and Provincial Treasurer. Other members of the Cabinet were C.W. Gross, Attorney-General; W.H. Cushing, Minister of Public Works; W.T. Finlay, Minister of Agriculture and Provincial Secretary; and Dr. L.G. DeVeber, Minister without Portfolio. Rutherford held the first election in November 1905, with the result that his Liberal government was sustained 23 to 2. The population of Alberta at this time was 73000 persons.

His first term as Premier was four years and he was again elected in 1909 on a slogan, "Rutherford and Railways", at which election the government was again sustained 37 to 4. However, he resigned the premiership on May 26, 1910, owing to dissension in the ranks of Liberal members of the Legislature. On his retirement, Lieutenant-Governor Bulyea called upon Chief Justice Arthur Sifton to fill the vacancy.

Under Rutherford administration the Normal School and the University of Alberta were founded. He was the first exponent of railway expansion of Alberta, guarantee on bonds, and he encouraged agriculture, coal mining, judicious labour legislation, and state control of telephones.

In 1913, Rutherford failed in his re-election bid, being defeated by Conservative H.H. Crawford, a Strathcona merchant. He then retired from active politics. In 1921, he came out of retirement to campaign on behalf of the Conservatives.

Widely read, Rutherford had a particularly extensive library of Canadian historical works. Always interested in education, he became known as the Father of the University of Alberta and was Chancellor of that institution from 1926 until his death. The Toronto Globe characterized him as "an honest, upright figure in politics. A big man physically and mentally with a radiant humour in his eyes, and lines of stubborn strength finely blended in his genial face."

Late in life he was awarded honorary degrees from his own university, McGill, as well as from Toronto, McMaster and Alberta. In 1889, he married Mattie Birkett of Ottawa. They had a son, Cecil, and a daughter, Hazel, who married Stanley H. McCuaig, an Edmonton lawyer. Religion: Baptist.

Arthur Sifton, *Second Premier of Alberta 1910-1917*

(See: List of Members of Parliament)

Charles Stewart, *Third Premier of Alberta 1917-1921*

(See: List of Members of Parliament)

Harry E. Strom, *Ninth Premier of Alberta 1969-1971*

Born July 7, 1914, at Burdett, Alberta, he was educated there and is of Scandinavian descent. He is a successful rancher. He was elected a municipal councillor when he was twenty-six, and has served on the Ballman School Board for many years. An active Christian layman in the Evangelical Free Church, he has long participated in the work of other Christian organizations and service groups. He has a long record of executive and teaching positions in his church.

At the age of forty-one in 1955, he entered provincial politics as the Social Credit candidate for the south-eastern constituency of Cypress. He was elected and entered Premier Manning's cabinet seven years later as Minister of Agriculture. He held this post for the next six years until he was transferred to Municipal Affairs in 1968.

Later the same year, Manning, who had sat in the Legislature for thirty-three years and had been Premier for the last twenty-five years, announced his plans to retire from politics. Strom was among the five Social Credit M.L.As who sought the position.

There was a feeling that, although Manning did not endorse any of the candidates, his blessed had been placed on the tall, soft-spoken, church-going southern Albertan rancher. Strom won the contest at a convention held in Edmonton in early December on the second ballot. He polled 915 votes compared to his nearest rival, Highways Minister Gordon Taylor who had 605. Six of Manning's cabinet had supported Strom.

It is interesting that fundamentalism should provide the link between all three social Cedi Premiers. Aberhart, Manning and Strom differed on many other measures such as ethnic, origin and type of education. Through Strom never engaged in the public evangelical activity of his predecessors, he is a strong member of a fundamentalist sect.

The new Premier was sworn in with his cabinet on December 10, 19168. More of a listener than a talker, Strom inclined away from publicity. He was fond of research and long-term detailed planning, but he lacked the charisma of leadership. He was a caretaker leader because he was in the Manning tradition. On one hand, Alfred Hooke, who he had not taken into his cabinet, as calling for a return to the Social Credit principles of Major Douglas, while on the other hand many were advocating a form of social conservatism.

The provincial general election as called for late August 1971, and even though Strom w=held his seat, the Social Credit party's representation in the

Legislature dropped from 55 out of 65 in the old Chamber to only 25 out of 75 in the new. The Conservatives, under the able leadership of Peter Lougheed, a Calgary lawyer, won a total of 49 seats. His main slogan was that it was time for a change. The remaining MLA is NDP-er, Grant Notley, who was elected in Spirit River.

Strom's leadership is currently in question. The support the party had as the government is starting to drain away. On June 2, 1972, SoCred Dr. Dana Bouvier of Lac La Biche, who had been first elected to the Legislature in a by-election in 1968, quit the party and announced he would sit as an Independent. Many of the present Social Credit Members of the Legislature are bureaucrats rather than parliamentarians. It is doubtful if Strom, who is now fifty-eight years of age, will lead the Social Credit party in the next provincial election which may be four years away. It is ironic that more people in Alberta voted for Social Credit candidates in 1971 than ever before, but it is uncertain whether the party will get anywhere near so many votes in the next election.

Henry Wise Wood, *President of the UFA 1916-1931*

(This is the only biographical sketch of an Albertan who was never elected to either the Legislature or sat in the federal Parliament. H.W. Wood, who was referred to as "The Moses of the Alberta Farmers", is too significant a figure to be omitted from this work.)

Born in 1860 on a farm near Monroe City, Missouri, he was the son of James Oliver Wood, a prosperous slave-owning farmer who served in the Confederate Army during the American Civil War. He attended the Christian University in Canton, Missouri, preparing for the ministry in the Campbellite sect. Though he did not enter the ministry, his study of the Bible, and especially the social teachings of Christ, exerted a profound influence on his thinking. He tilled the soil in his home state, then migrated to Texas where became a cotton planter. Returning to Missouri, he again engaged in farming. His tuition in agrarian politics was largely obtained in the Farmer's Equity Movement in the mid-west in the 1890s.

Attracted to Canada in 1905, Wood, at the age of forty-five, obtained a farm in the Carstairs district of central Alberta. He never gave up his American citizenship. He became actively interested in the farmer's movement in his community. In 1909, he joined the recently-organized United Farmers of Albreta and became the UFA president seven years later. In 1917, Prime Minister Borden asked him to join the Union government as Minister of Agriculture. He refused.

It was under his careful guidance that the farmers' political movement developed in Alberta. After the provincial election of 1921, UFA candidates had won a total of 39 seats in the 60 Member Legislature. Wood was offered the premiership. Much to the surprise of his political opponents, he declined the office, preferring to remain the UFA president. His associate, Herbert Greenfield, was chosen Premier by the UFA Members of the Legislature. Henry Wise Wood was the most outstanding figure, politically and economically, the agrarian movement in western Canada produced. He was the directing spirit of the UFA until his retired from the presidency in 1931. By virtue of his position, he was often described as exercising a subtle but beneficent "dictatorship" as regards his relations with the farmers' government in Edmonton.

Some 30000 Alberta farmers united into a solid group under Wood's leadership and wielded tremendous political power as a "class" group. The UFA dominated provincial politics for fourteen years until the Social Credit were swept into office in 1935. A strong believer in cooperation, he was chairman of the Alberta Wheat Pool, 1923-1937. The University of Alberta conferred upon him the honorary Doctor of Laws in 1929. Wood died at the age of eighty-one in Calgary in 1941.

Epilogue

More and more Canadians are realizing that knowledge of their own history and experience is essential to a sense of regional and national identity. The aim of this work has been to make certain facts regarding the men sent from the Province of Alberta to Ottawa known. It is hoped that as a result, we will have a greater understanding of the forces that are working within confederation.

A further study is currently underway on the Alberta Legislative Assembly since 1905. A total of 505 Albertans have been elected to the provincial House.

www.ingramcontent.com/pod-product-compliance
Lightning Source LLC
Chambersburg PA
CBHW031553300426
44111CB00006BA/303